SERVING WITH THE BLUES

First published in 2006 by

WOODFIELD PUBLISHING
Bognor Regis, West Sussex, England
www.woodfieldpublishing.com

ISBN 1-84683-011-7

Serving with
the Blues

*Adventures of a former RAF Bandsman
and Jazz Musician at Home and Abroad*

PETER BRADBURY

Woodfield

Evacuated!

To my wife Pauline
and daughters
Debbie, Amanda, Rachel and Caroline

Contents

Introduction

This is a true story about a small boy evacuated to Lancashire at the beginning of World War II, the only difference between me and other evacuees being that I lived with my Great Aunt, Betsy Jackson and her family.

This is also a story of my struggle to achieve recognition as a professional musician and follow in my father's footsteps, something not many offspring choose to do these days...

1. Early Years

I was born in Weymouth, Dorset in the year 1935. My father Tommy was a professional musician and my mother Rachel a professional ballroom dancer. Until the age of three I lived with them in Sweden. My parents were both excellent skiers, and used to take me with them, even at that tender age I skied down the slopes with some considerable skill. Dad played with a dance band at the Grand Hotel, Stockholm and Mum gave dancing exhibitions with her partner.

The Second World War broke out in 1939 and I was evacuated to the small town of Bacup in Lancashire, to live with my Great Aunt Betsy, her husband Walt and Great Cousin Ruth. Bacup is situated in the Rossendale Valley, the home of 'Slipper Mills', it is an extremely compact little town, typical of old Lancashire, with hills, cobblestone roads and very few pavements. Betsy and Walt had a bungalow situated at the top of one of those steep 'brews', which went by the name of Thorn Hill.

One cold wintry morning Mum and Dad put me onto a train at King's Cross station, along with a couple of suitcases, and a label tied around my neck with my destination on it. Mum asked the Guard to keep an eye on me, to which the kindly old fellow agreed – after all, a little chap of three and a half tender years could hardly take care of himself on a journey of two-hundred miles, could he? Aunt Betsy and Uncle Walt came to meet me at Piccadilly Station, Manchester, then the three of us boarded a bus bound for Rochdale, then changed to another one to Bacup. By the time we had alighted, darkness descended on us.

I had disappeared into a deep sleep, so Walt had to pick me up and carry me.

"How are you going to carry Peter up the brew?" Aunt Betsy asked.

"I'll manage," Walt answered.

When we arrived at 'The Bungalow', Ruth, my seventeen-year-old cousin greeted us.

"Phew!" Walt gasped, "I 've lived 'ere all m'life, but I swear t'brews git steeper!"

"Don't forget that you've had a little package to carry," Aunt Betsy said, jovially.

That's true," Uncle Walt replied, "But he's worth it!"

"What a bonny lad," Ruth remarked, "Such a shame to have to leave his Mum and Dad."

"T'is better'n bein' bombed i' London," Walt said (the Bradbury family had moved from Sweden to London just before the outbreak of the Second World War, which unfortunately turned out to be a bad move!).

"That's true," Aunt Betsy agreed, then went off to make some tea.

Although prior to living in London I had lived in Sweden, where the temperature always read below zero, the 'Frozen North', that's a different story. Whereas in Sweden where the sun shone and the air fresh and clean, the smoke from the mills and factories, and freezing cold in Lancashire, were a lot to contend with. Nevertheless, with a kind Aunt, Uncle and Cousin to look after me, I felt quite contented, even though I missed my Mum and Dad.

I had just reached my fourth birthday, and the time had arrived for me to go to school.

"That is going to be a problem," Auntie told me, "Uncle goes to work at five o'clock in the morning, Ruth goes at six, and your school is right down at the bottom of the Brew.

"Can't you take me Auntie?" I asked her.

"Auntie has bad legs due to an accident caused by a car a few years ago. I find it difficult to manage to climb up 'The Brew'," Auntie answered.

It made me feel extremely sad to hear that, and I said reassuringly, "Don't worry Auntie, I will go by myself."

As luck would have it, there lived an Irish family named O'Shaunessy in the bungalow across the way. As soon as she heard of the problem, 'cheery-faced Bridget' (as she had become affectionately known to her friends) had the solution. Three of her children went to the infants' school, and as she had older children, they could take me to school with them.

"Oh, that is kind," Auntie said, "Thank you very much. Thank goodness Peter will have friends already, as he is so far away from home."

As we sat in front of the black lead stove, drinking our cups of tea, Auntie said to Uncle Walt, "What a relief! That is a load off my mind."

"I agree," Walt answered, then went on somewhat ruefully, "T'trouble is, t'O'Shaunessy young'ns are ruffuns"

"You really must try to speak more clearly," Betsy scolded him, "or Peter will not be able to understand you!"

"T'is t'way I was brung up,", he answered gruffly, then went on,"I c'n 'ardly understand Cockneys anyroad."

"He wasn't born within the sound of Bow Bells," Betsy corrected him.

"They all sound t'same t'me," Walt mumbled.

School became a dramatic experience for me. Although I was far from home, and had been pushed from pillar to post, I had too soft a nature to be thrown into a rough situation like that one. The school was aptly named 'Thorn' and was a tough place. Being a Londoner and quiet, the local children accused me of being a snob, so inevitably they bullied me. Luckily, Sean, the ten-year-old elder of the O'Shaunessy boys (and also really tough) and I had struck up a close relationship and if any bullies tried to pick on me, Sean would appear and stick up for me.

One summer's day, while walking home from school with Sean, we were almost there when Sean said, "Me Ma's expectin' me 'ome early, you'll be a'reet on tha' sen now?"

"Of course I will," I answered, then went off on my own for a stroll in the nearby field.

A little voice behind me made me jump.

"Hello, who are you?"

I turned around, and there in front of me stood a little girl. She was beautiful, about the same age as myself, maybe a couple of months younger. She had long auburn hair and the most beautiful hazel eyes I had ever seen.

"Good evening," I said, smiling at her, "I'm Peter, what's your name?"

"Lottie," she answered. "My goodness you are posh, aren't you?"

"Posh!" I retorted, "What's that mean?"

Lottie thought for a moment before answering.

"I'm sorry, I didn't mean to offend you, but most of the other children around here speak strangely, and I can't understand what they say, but you have a beautiful voice."

I blushed right down to my toes, "Thank you," I stuttered, "And where do you come from, Lottie?"

"Not far from you, Hackney, in the East End of London," she replied.

"We were almost neighbours then," I said.

We walked for ages, chatting and picking daisies. Suddenly a man's voice boomed behind us, "Hey there young'un, Auntie's bin worrit baht thee," Uncle Walt said.

"I'm sorry to worry Auntie," I said apologetically.

"Tha's reet," Uncle Walt laughed.

"I met my friend Lottie and we lost track of time."

"Let's tak' 'er w'om then," Walt said.

"Yes," I answered, "We will take you home first, Lottie." We took Lottie to her front door, explained to her Auntie, then went home.

Lottie lived in the road adjacent to us, so I would be seeing quite a lot of her.

We had 'jam butties' for tea, followed by cakes, with ice-cream to finish, a special treat because, by any standards, Auntie and Uncle were quite poor. Jam Butties were going to form a large part of my diet from then on, but I didn't mind that because I had people who loved me, that was the main thing – I thought so, anyway.

The next day was Saturday and Uncle Walt, following his usual routine, brought me a mug of tea and a jam buttie at 4am. I tried to open my eyes, but couldn't. I could hear Walt in the distance, raking the ashes from the fireplace and stove, busying himself by getting ready for work. I opened my eyes, looked at the little night-light flickering in the dark, pulled aside the curtains and shivered.

A thick frost covered the moors, and I could see the smoke from the chimneys, spiralling up to the sky, and the moon casting weird shadows.

'Oh... quite eerie!' It can't be daytime already," I said out loud. I had become accustomed to waking up in the daylight but I had a different life to lead now. I thought of Mummy and Daddy with tears in my eyes, but when Auntie came and kissed me and told me not to be afraid, everything seemed all right.

I enjoyed the hot mug of tea and the thick crust of homemade bread, smothered with jam. 'What a funny taste', I thought, but I didn't realise that there wasn't any butter, only margarine, and I'd never tasted that before. I closed my eyes and fell into a deep sleep once more.

I awakened to find Auntie gently shaking my shoulder.

"Wake up Peter, it's 8 o'clock."

"Yes Auntie, thank you," I answered sleepily.

"What are you thanking me for?" she asked.

"Oh… for both you and Uncle taking the place of Mummy and Daddy, looking after me," I explained.

She answered with that soft voice that I had come to know and love so well.

"No-one can ever take the place of your parents, but we will do everything in our power to make you happy."

"I am happy already," I assured her, but I didn't realise at that time just how happy I had made my three relatives.

Cousin Ruth worked until lunchtime, Uncle also, so while Auntie busied herself in the kitchen, I said, "Can I do anything to help you?"

"I do need two bottles of sterilized milk," she replied, "And if you will take these two empties back, you can keep the money deposited on the bottles."

As she couldn't afford to give me pocket-money, it was the only way that she could think of, until money arrived from my Daddy.

"You know the little shop at the bottom of 'The Brew', but be careful not to fall, as it is extremely steep," she warned.

"I will be careful," I replied.

I ran down the cobblestone hill, so excited that I forgot Auntie's warning. Suddenly over I went, and as the bottles smashed I felt pain, and the blood running down my arms and legs… then nothing…

Sean and his brother and sisters were playing in the garden when they heard the crash and smash of bottles, and my screams.

"Oh my goodness!" Sean exclaimed, and rushed down the hill. He picked me up in his arms, as if lifting a small baby. Although only a few years older than me, he had the strength of an ox. He rushed into the little shop and called out,

"Somebody please help me, poor Peter has fallen, and I'm afraid that there are pieces of glass in his arms and legs."

The shopkeeper cleaned my wounds as best she could, picking out the bits of glass, and bandaging me up, while her husband phoned for the ambulance. Meanwhile, Sean rushed to tell Auntie Betsy what had happened.

Uncle worked in the 'Felt Works' at Waterfoot, just a couple of miles from their home. He met Ruth at the bus stop as usual, and they were just about to start up the hill, when the ambulance stopped, and the driver quickly told them what had happened. They all rushed off to Bury Infirmary, some ten miles away. Luckily for me, no real damage had been done, but I did have stitches in both of my forearms and legs. I would carry those scars for the rest of my life, but there would be worse knocks than that in the future.

I spent only one day in hospital, but that was enough for me. I certainly would have to be more careful in the future. When I arrived back home at Auntie's, I felt like an 'Egyptian Mummy', with bandages around both arms and legs. Ruth laughed at me, but only jokingly, as she wouldn't have hurt my feelings for anything! My wounds soon healed, and I felt like my old self again in next to no time.

Each Saturday, I went with Auntie Betsy and Ruth to the cinema. On the way home Auntie would buy a bag of chips, and we would sit listening to the radio, or playing games. Uncle Walt, the local snooker and billiards champion, would walk with us to the pictures, then meet us afterwards. That became a regular occurrence until I reached my eighth birthday, then Uncle asked me to go to the billiard-hall with him.

"Oh yes please!" I answered full of excitement.

"You don't want to go to that smelly place, do you Peter?" Auntie asked, "It is extremely smoky, and the people aren't all that pleasant."

"Uncle will look after me," I replied.

Before long I had grasped the basics of both snooker and billiards. Uncle had the knack of passing on his skill to others. Auntie had got one thing right though ugh!... the peculiar smell.

"Uncle," I began, one evening while we were at the 'Hall', "...Why do you always have a cigarette in your mouth?"

"T'is just a bad habit Peter lad," Walt answered, "I don't inhale, just k'ep 'n b'rn'ng in m'mouth all t'time."

"Is that why you have a bad cough?" I asked.

"Yes I'm 'fraid t'is," he replied again.

Uncle always had a cigarette dangling from his lips. I hadn't meant to be rude, but it worried me to think of Uncle becoming ill. I could not for the life of me understand why, if it made him cough, did he smoke? I would learn why later on in life.

One day a letter came from my Mummy and Daddy, to say that Daddy would be appearing with the 'Squadronaires Royal Air Force Dance Band' at the Astoria, Rawtenstall. Daddy would be visiting me, and as I hadn't seen either of my parents for two years, I felt really excited.

"I do wish that I could see Mummy also," I said to Auntie.

"Unfortunately," she replied, "Due to the war, with Daddy being in the RAF, Mummy has to stay in London and is not able to be with him."

"I do miss them both," I remarked, sadly.

"Never mind," Auntie replied, and to cheer me up said, "At least you will see your Daddy next week."

I felt delighted, but unfortunately the day before Tommy came to see me I suffered a terrible toothache. By the time that he had arrived, I could hardly talk for the pain. The thought of going to the dentist frightened me, but Daddy said, "If you will let me take you to the dentist, I will buy something exciting for you."

"I would love a 'draughts set' please Daddy," I said.

"That's what you'll have then," Tommy answered.

The visit to the dentist went off without a hitch, I had a bad tooth extracted, and my Daddy bought a draughts set for me, which I kept until my thirty-fifth birthday, when it became 'lost in transit' somehow.

In the whole of my young life until I met my future wife Pauline, the time spent with Auntie and her family gave me much happiness. Although I was unaware of the fact at the time, music would play an extremely important part of my future life, but would also make me unhappier than anything else … well at times, anyway.

Daddy stayed for one week, and Auntie, Uncle and Ruth took me to the Astoria Ballroom to hear him play. We went every evening, and each performance seemed better than the previous one. It gave me a thrill to see him sitting there in his smart blue RAF uniform, and made me feel really proud.

'That's my Daddy!"

There were nineteen members of the 'Squadronaires' dance orchestra: 2 Alto Saxophones 2 Tenor Saxophones 1 Baritone Saxophone, 4 Bb Trumpets, 4 Slide Trombones. Rhythm Section: Piano, String Bass, Drums, Guitar. Then there was the Leader/Vocalist Female Vocalist.

When my Daddy stood up to take a jazz solo, I couldn't restrain myself, I just clapped and cheered, mind you I wasn't the only one! During the interval, Daddy introduced some members of the orchestra to me. Most of them had gone to the bar for a beer, but the '4 Teetotallers' were in the restaurant, so I made conversation with them,

"Will I be able to play as well as you, when I grow up?" I asked Andy McDevitt the 2nd altoist.

"If you work hard and practise every day, yes of course," Andy replied, then continued, "Mind you, a saxophone would be useful. The best instrument for you, until you grow a bit bigger, is a clarinet. Why don't you ask your Dad to buy one for you?"

"I don't think that Daddy can afford one, but I'll ask him," I answered.

That remark amused the musicians.

"I wish that my children were so considerate," Andy said with a smirk on his face. The others agreed with him.

Kenny Baker, the third trumpeter, later to become one of the most famous jazz trumpet players in England, if not in the world, said to me, "I thought you played the violin, Peter."

"I have a three-quarter-size one, which Daddy bought for me," I replied, "I took lessons for two years, but with the terrible screeching sound and 'I thought that someone had trodden on the cat!' remarks, also other children calling me a 'cissy' as I walked through the streets carrying my instrument, I gave it up."

"Peter," Jimmy Durant, the baritone sax player said, "I agree with Andy, I also think that you should start with the clarinet."

"I will ask Daddy, anyway." I decided.

I would remember the 'Four Tea Drinkers' for years to come. Every time I went with my Daddy to rehearsals I ended up chatting to them. It had been wonderful to see Daddy again, and I knew that I would be most upset when he went away once more.

The evening of the final performance arrived, Tommy purchased tickets for Auntie, Uncle, Ruth, also Sean and family. Oh! and one for Lottie. My friends were most impressed. Lottie held my hand during the performance.

"That will be you one day," she said, in a dreamy voice, "I can just see you standing there, in your smart blue uniform, playing your saxophone 'Gosh, you do look smart and handsome!"

"Well…" I replied, "I don't know whether I fancy wearing a uniform or not Lottie, but I do fancy playing the saxophone."

After the concert we all went to a party. At midnight Uncle Walt said, "How are we going to get home?" Daddy suggested a taxi, "It is Saturday night, surely nobody has to get up early in the morning, do they?" he asked.

We all shook our heads, then stayed on until 2am. We had a great time at the party, and I met hundreds of people, most of them from 'Show Business'. I had a glass of punch, so did Lottie and Sean. We all ended up a little bit tipsy by the end of the party. There were lots of records of the popular bands of that era. The Disc Jockey put on a waltz, and Lottie said to me, "Will you dance with me?" That took me aback, I had never in my life danced before.

"I don't know how to dance Lottie," I said nervously.

"I will show you," she offered, laughing, "Don't be afraid," and she dragged me onto the dance-floor.

I felt quite silly, I didn't wish to be laughed at again, I had quite enough of that when playing the violin.

"Oh all right then," I answered grumpily, "But don't do any of those fancy steps, will you?"

"I won't," Lottie promised, snuggling up to me, and that made me feel warm and relaxed.

The next dance was a jitterbug, and even though I could not dance all that well, the rhythm in me made my feet tap, and suddenly I was dancing as if I had been doing it for years.

"That was marvellous," Lottie said after the dance, "Where did you learn to dance like that?"

"I didn't," I assured her, "It just came naturally."

"Maybe you should become a dancer!" Lottie teased.

I just laughed, the idea of becoming a dancer amused me. By that time my stomach let me know that it needed food. I looked at the buffet, there were… sandwiches… cakes… and virtually anything that one could wish for.

After the party, the taxi dropped Lottie off first, then Sean and his family, then Auntie and the rest of us. I fell asleep as soon as my head hit the pillow, but Tommy, Auntie Betsy, Uncle and Ruth chatted for a couple of hours, mostly about my future.

"We are going to Ireland tomorrow," Tommy said, "With Frankie Lane for approximately six months. I will write to you as soon as soon as we return to London."

Although I felt sad at Daddy's departure, it didn't upset me as much as I had expected, probably due to the fact of living at Auntie's for some time.

We had been fairly lucky in the country, especially as far as the bombing. The major cities were badly hit, for example Manchester, Birmingham and Leeds, but compared with London – nothing really. Even so, there had been many close calls for my relatives and myself. For instance, one Saturday afternoon, after one of our regular trips to the cinema, we had bought our chips as usual and were just boarding the bus for Bacup when the air-raid-siren sounded, wailing horrifyingly, followed by a terrific explosion. When the dust settled we realised that the cinema we had just visited had completely disappeared, along with every other building surrounding it. What a frightening experience! The memory would stay in my mind forever. There were also a few times when we had to make a dash for the air-raid-shelter, but all-in-all, we were fairly lucky.

The time would soon be approaching for me to leave Lancashire and return to my parents in London. Auntie Betsy could hardly bear to think of that, so she didn't mention it to me until the day arrived. I had reached my tenth birthday, and the end of the war was at hand.

Cousin Ruth had started 'going steady' with a new boyfriend. I liked Alan. He used to come to see Ruth every evening and sometimes when they weren't going out he would play games with me. Sometimes Ruth and Alan took Aunt Betsy and me to the pictures, or on a coach trip to Blackpool. Alan even bought me a 'Meccano' set, which the two of us spent many happy hours playing with.

One of the main highlights of my life 'up North', was the once yearly holiday at Blackpool, the one thing that even Uncle Walt stopped working for.

"Come on Peter love," Auntie would say, shaking me gently, "Wake up. It's Blackpool day!"

I didn't need any further coaxing, jumping out of bed, dressing myself, almost as quickly as you could blink. Considering the fact that Uncle didn't own a car, it truly is amazing how we ever arrived at Blackpool at all. What with the cases, bags and particularly my buckets and spades, poor Uncle was like a pack-horse. Occasionally we travelled to Blackpool by bus or train, but the usual method was by charabanc.

It so happened, that one particular holiday at Blackpool, I nearly frightened Auntie and Uncle 'out of their wits'. Uncle gathered the luggage and then we made our way to the Yelloway Coach Station. Once we were settled into our seats, the coach left the terminus for its destination. The journey took approximately three hours, quite a long time to sit in one position, but there were a few stops en-route to allow passengers to stretch their legs and take refreshments.

At long last we reached our destination. The sun shone brightly as we left the coach, but with quite a fierce wind. I shivered and pulled my balaclava over my head. We reached the boarding house, signed in, then washed and changed into suitable clothes for the beach.

As we walked past the penny slot machine arcade I said, "Uncle, can we go in there?"

Uncle looked at me and smiled.

"Well Lad, just f'r t'short while," he said, "We don't want t' spend all 'r money on t'first day, do we?"

"No Uncle," I agreed with him.

There were people hustling and bustling and rushing and pushing, pulling levers on various machines and generally feeding coins into them as if there was no tomorrow. I was about to insert a penny piece into my favourite hand-grabber that picked up little trinkets, then dropped them down a chute, when someone jostled me and I dropped my penny. As I bent to pick it up, a man knocked me to the ground. As I picked myself up, I turned around to see where Auntie and Uncle were, but they were nowhere to be seen. My heart nearly missed a beat. I felt like a midget among a crowd of giants, after all, a seven-year-old in not very big.

I fought my way to the exit, then looked around for Auntie and Uncle. 'Oh dear!' I thought, 'Where can they be?' I had just started to tell an attendant of my predicament when a familiar voice called out to me.

"Peter lad, tha' nearly skeered's t'deeth."

Uncle Walt certainly seemed relieved to see me.

"I'm sorry Uncle, I got lost in the crowd," I replied.

"I hope you haven't spent all your money," Auntie said.

Much to her relief, I confirmed that I had not done so.

We took a ride in an open-top tram along the promenade to the fairground, where my favourite ride was the Big Dipper, even though the top of it hid behind clouds and the steep slopes were quite scary. Auntie waited while we three daredevils went for a ride on it. Uncle paid the attendant sixpence for each of us and we settled safely in our seats. The safety bar was fastened across us and the car moved slowly forward. As it started to move I felt a tingle of excitement running up and down my spine and 'butterflies' in my tummy. The car rattled noisily up the steep incline, then once at the summit, ran down the track, gathering speed as it went, leaving my stomach behind.

After the ride, the three of us scrambled out of the car and I ran excitedly to Auntie.

"Gosh! That felt great, can we go up again, Auntie?"

"Not today dear, there will be plenty of time later," she replied, firmly but softly.

"I know…" I suggested, "Let's go to see 'The Laughing Man'.

The famous 'Laughing Man' had been at the fairground at Blackpool for years. He was just a dummy in a glass case, and after inserting a penny piece one would hear a rib-tickling laugh that could make even the most serious-minded person erupt into fits of laughter. I fed my penny into the slot and stood back. The smirk on the dummy's face broke into a grin and his giggles turned into laughter, then finally into guffaws and tears rolled down his cheeks.

"Come on now lad," Uncle interrupted the mirth making, "T'is time f'r summat to eat."

We found a fish and chip bar, and sat down to a good feed.

The boarding house, although small, looked neat and tidy. The landlady was a fat, jovial lady to whom I had taken an instant liking. At breakfast time she gave me an extra slice of my favourite, bacon.

On the last day of the holiday I went with Auntie and Uncle to the beach. The sun was particularly hot with not even a breeze. I busied myself building a sandcastle and Uncle dug out a moat while Auntie relaxed in a deckchair, taking in the sun. Suddenly I heard a clinking sound as my metal spade struck something.

'I Wonder what that can be?' I said.

"Hey Uncle!" I called out, "I've found something."

Uncle Walt came over to see what all the fuss was about, and then proceeded to help me to dig the object out of the sand. Whatever it was, it seemed quite large. Gradually, as we removed the sand, the article took shape – an urn, most definitely silver, extremely old and most certainly valuable.

"What's that doing under the sand, Uncle?" I asked.

"I don't know," Walt replied, "But one thing's f'r sure, t'as bin th're a long time."

The urn was beautifully ornamented, with serpents round the neck and a dragon around the base.

"T'is probably part of a burglary," Uncle decided, "We'd better tak' it to t' Police Station."

I felt really excited. "Perhaps it comes from a city under the sea," I gabbled, "Maybe Atlantis!"

Auntie and Uncle both laughed at me.

"What an imagination," Uncle said, hugging me.

The local Police Station was crowded and the desk-sergeant busy writing. Uncle walked up to him.

"Excuse me officer," he said.

The sergeant looked up wearily from his work.

"Good morning sir, can I help you?" he offered.

"We have found this urn on the beach," Uncle explained, "Will you take charge of it?"

Suddenly the policeman sat up.

"Will you step this way sir?" he asked. "I will have to ask you a few questions."

Auntie and I sat down in the waiting-room while Uncle went with the sergeant, who asked a few questions and made notes.

"You say you dug this up from under the sand sir?" he began.

Walt answered affirmatively.

After leaving his home address with the desk-sergeant, Walt took hold of my hand and went with Auntie, back to the beach.

Some months later, we were contacted by the police, who informed us that the urn was part of a shipload of antiques that had been wrecked offshore some years previously. There was a reward of £200 for the return of the missing urn, so Uncle would be entitled to it. What a happy end to a very exciting holiday at Blackpool!

Football and cricket matches were the other regular events which Uncle and I enjoyed, and as he was the secretary of Bacup Borough Football and Cricket Club there were plenty of free tickets to be had. When Bacup played away, Uncle and I would take a pile of sandwiches and a flask of coffee, travel with the team on the coach and have a terrific day out. Usually it was freezing while watching the game, but with the excitement and the refreshments, neither Uncle nor I seemed to notice it.

Eventually the dreaded day arrived when I had to go home to my Mum and Dad. The year was 1947 and I had reached my twelfth birthday. Mum and Dad had been to see me at Auntie's a couple of times. Of course, they wanted me to go home with them, but strangely enough I didn't want to go, and neither did Auntie, Uncle or Ruth want me to. So began the big controversy. My dad, Tommy still travelled all over the world, and my mum Rachel, now that the war had ended, moved around with him.

"Wouldn't he be better off staying with us?" Auntie asked Mum and Dad. "You could come to see him as often as you wished."

My Dad agreed but Mum objected quite strongly.

"He is our son, not yours," she said to Auntie.

That final remark of Mum's really upset me. I realised that during the war I had to be evacuated somewhere, but to my way of thinking if Mum hadn't bothered to come to see me during those many years and didn't even write to me, how could she possibly love me as much as she made out.

I aired my views strongly, but to no avail, and so it was that I returned to London...

Author with Great Aunt Betsy.

Great Uncle Walt with Bacup Borough FC, 1946.

Great Cousin Ruth.

Cousin Ruth on her wedding day to Ronnie Moss.

The Squadronaires Dance Orchestra, Dad second from left.

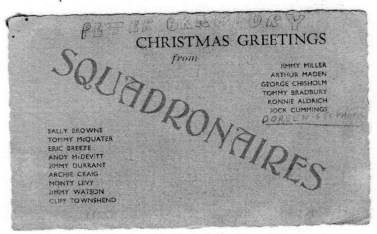

Squadronaires card.

My Dad, Tommy.

My Mum Rachel with sister Christine and Rufus.

2. Teenage Years

I returned to London the same way I had left it almost nine years before, on my own. Mum and Dad met me at King's Cross Station in a taxi. I felt absolutely lost, feeling terribly upset about leaving Aunt Betsy, Uncle Walt and Ruth but looking forward, in a way, to seeing my Mum and Dad again. I had very mixed feelings and now that I had reached the ripe old age of twelve, I felt I had a right to have a say as to where I lived and with whom.

We arrived at the flat in Neasden and, as I had been travelling for the best part of the day, I felt exhausted. The three of us climbed the steps (oh those steps!) and it seemed an eternity before we reached No.6 on the top floor.

"If only we had a lift!" Mum and Dad puffed in unison.

The sound of barking greeted us as we approached the front door. Our dog Lucky (a large, three-year-old crossbred Retriever/Setter) waited to greet us. Dad had mentioned the dog on his last visit to Auntie's house.

"Be quiet Lucky!" Mum shouted, as the dog jumped up, nearly bowling me over. The animal had a great deal of strength, but was very affectionate.

Mum showed me to my bedroom and I went straight to bed, falling asleep as soon as my head touched the pillow.

We spent the next day unpacking and chatting. Dad had all-day rehearsals at Lime Grove Studios, Shepherds Bush, then a concert in the evening. Mum and I would be going later.

'That sounds exciting', I thought.

The concert was just one of many events I attended during the following few weeks until I started school again, I also travelled a lot. That evening Mum and I took the trolleybus from Neasden to Scrubs Lane, then changed to another for Shepherds Bush. We arrived early, so decided to have a snack in the restaurant nearby. Most of the musicians were there with their wives. They included Andy, Kenny and Jimmy Durant. George Chisholm (trombone) completed the line-up of 'tea drinkers'. They were all pleased to see me.

"Hell there, how's the fiddle playing going, Peter?" Andy asked jokingly.

"I haven't touched it, Andy," I replied with a grin, "It always sounds as if someone's treading on the cat!" They all laughed at that remark, remembering that I had said the same thing, when we last met.

"Did you speak to your Dad about getting a clarinet?" George asked me.

Mum looked at me and said, "You didn't say that you wanted to play the clarinet, Peter."

"I forgot, Mum, I responded, "Anyway, I'm sure that Dad can't afford it."

What a fantastic evening! Temporarily I had forgotten how upset I had become at leaving Auntie behind in Lancashire. We took our seats in the studio ten minutes before the performance was due to start, at eight o'clock.

Hughie Green took the stand and said, "Good evening Ladies and Gentlemen, welcome to a special concert to celebrate two years of 'world peace'. There are two lights above the entrance. Keep your eyes on them and when the amber one lights up, that is a warning that we will be on the air." I kept my eyes on the amber light... then suddenly the red one flashed and the live broadcast commenced.

Hughie made the announcement: "Presenting the Squadronaires Royal Air Force Dance Orchestra, playing themselves in with their signature tune: 'There's Something in the Air'.

Everyone clapped and cheered, the air was electric, and me? I couldn't sit still for the excitement. The next number was one of my favourites, Glen Miller's 'Little Brown Jug'. After that a comedy number, 'The Waiter and the Porter and the Upstairs Maid' featuring George Chisholm, Susan Jeans [vocalist] and Jimmy Miller [leader of the orchestra and male vocalist], that made the audience laugh. Next was Glen Miller's signature tune 'Moonlight Serenade'. Another one of my favourites followed, 'Anchors Aweigh', featuring Andy McDevitt on clarinet in a typically Benny Goodman style. Then, at long last, the moment I had been patiently waiting for: 'Smoke Gets in Your Eyes' featuring my Dad, Tommy Bradbury. I was enthralled and sat back, closing my eyes and imagining myself playing it. The next number was 'Slow Boat to China' featuring the Squadcats [Jimmy Miller, Susan Jeans and Harry Firth-Archer on the string bass]. Finally the Squadronaires signed off with their signature tune to finish the broadcast but after a short interval there would be more music, just for the audience. Mum and Dad went to the bar with some of the musicians, but I knew where I wished to go – to the restaurant with Andy and the 'Tea Drinkers'.

"This is a repeat performance of the Astoria at Rawtenstall," Andy said.

"Yes I answered, "and I would lay a bet that the conversation will be just as interesting." It certainly was, and I felt sad at the end of it.

The second half of the performance had the audience jumping up and down in their seats as they could relax now that the broadcast had finished. The Dixieland Session starred Andy on clarinet once more, with George on trombone, Jimmy the lead trumpet, Ronnie Aldrich on piano, Sid on guitar and last but not least Jock Cummins on drums.

Unfortunately the show had to end sometime, and it did eventually, at one o'clock in the morning, when Mum, Dad and I took a taxi home to put the finishing touch to a perfect evening.

For six months, I went to Braintcroft Junior School for day students. The school was situated near to my home in Neasden, which meant that I could continue to have some exciting times, at least when my Dad came home.

One day my Mum said to me, "How would you like to go to boarding school Peter?" I had just become accustomed to being home in London again with my parents, therefore the idea of going away again did not appeal to me at all.

"Why do you want to send me away again?" I asked her.

"It is not that I want to dear," she answered, "But Daddy has to go away for quite a while, and he wishes me to go with him."

"I don't want to go away again," I retorted angrily, "Unless you send me to Auntie's."

"That is not possible darling," my Mother answered finally.

That evening Dad had a word with me.

"You really would enjoy boarding-school, it is lots of fun, with pillow-fights and boys of your own age going on picnics and days out." Auntie and I wrote to each other every week, and when I told her about being sent away to boarding-school she became extremely angry. Uncle had plenty to say about it also.

"What's t'point o' takin' 'im away fro' us, where 'e w's 'appy, on'y t' send 'im t'boarding-school?" he said, lapsing into his heavy dialect again. He always did that when something annoyed him.

"I honestly don't know," Auntie Betsy answered, "But I think it's a right shame!"

"Tha's reet," Walt retorted, "But there's nowt we c'n do 'bout it."

Aunt Betsy and Uncle Walt had wanted to adopt me years before, but my Mum and Dad wouldn't hear of it.

Eventually, I was persuaded to go to boarding school at Harrow, where I remained, holidays excepted, for two long years. That really was a shock to my system, particularly as I expected it to be fun, after all that my Dad had told me, when in fact it turned out to be quite the opposite.

The only good thing to come out of my time spent at boarding school was that I learned to play the piano.

Mr Hodges the Headmaster showed himself to be a strict disciplinarian, one of his faults being that he had favourites, and I certainly did not become one of them. He used to wield a thick, heavy walking stick and his favourite way to punish rule-breakers was by using it across our bottoms when we were in our pyjamas. I had good cause to remember that stick, unfortunately!

I didn't do all that well at lessons, except French, which became one of my main interests. The school day began by getting out of bed at six, making up our beds, then down to the Great Hall for breakfast. Lessons were from nine until midday, with an hour and a half for lunch, then lessons again until 4:30. After school, dinner, homework, then to bed at 9pm and lights out at 9.30.

The only highlight of my life at boarding school, other than French and piano lessons, was Matron making cups of cocoa at 8pm each evening. We pupils used to take a couple of slices of bread from the dining-hall and toast them on the electric fire in the rest room, then we would spread them with margarine and pretend we were eating toast and butter.

Mr Hodges used to take his 'favourites' to the theatre in the West End of London once a week. He had four favourite pupils, who were all dislikeable characters. As for pillow-fights, we didn't dare for fear of 'The Stick'.

One of the headmaster's 'pets' nearly had me expelled. One hot summer's day we were playing in the vast garden behind the college in our swimming trunks. We were being sprayed with a hosepipe by Mr Hodges when the number one favourite and bully Horace Entwistle pulled down my trunks and pushed me over. The bully was twice my size, but didn't reckon with my temper. Before I realised what I was doing I picked up a brick and threw it at Horace. The bully ducked but the brick hit him on the arm, breaking the bone. The bully, in tears, wailed at me and threatened to get even. Needless to say, I received the stick, but after I had explained why I had thrown the brick, much to my surprise, the bully also received a walloping.

The summer holidays arrived and the college closed down for eight weeks. I had received two letters from my parents during the course of the six months I had been away, though admittedly they had been touring around much of the time.

The holiday would turn out to be really exciting. The Squadronaires were playing at Butlins Holiday Camp, Clacton-on-Sea and I would be spending the whole of my break there. Although I didn't know it at the time, I would be meeting Lottie again, this time at Clacton.

Mum picked me up from the college and we went home to pack. Dad was already there when we arrived and, after gathering all our things, we clambered into 'Cuvvie' (Mum had given the car that nickname because of the registration CUV) and had a pleasant drive through the countryside. Being a reliable old vehicle, it transported the three of us to Clacton without incident.

On arrival at Butlins we went directly to our chalet and unpacked. The chalets were like tiny bungalows, blue and yellow in colour and reasonably comfortable. I found plenty to occupy myself with at the camp, and besides enjoying myself, I soon found a way of earning some pocket money. The entertainment staff were called 'Redcoats' for obvious reasons and my best school blazer, also being red in colour, would serve a very useful purpose. Each Saturday morning as the campers were booking in I would seize the opportunity to offer my services.

"Can I show you to your chalet Sir and help you with some of the lighter luggage?"

This usually resulted in my receiving sixpence or a shilling, and sometimes, if I was really lucky, as much as two shillings. Some weeks I earned as much as £2 – a fortune to a small boy, and my savings soon mounted.

After I had finished earning my pocket money I would go to the main ballroom to see my friends. The ballroom had other uses during the day, for example talent contests, beauty competitions and so on… By now I had made lots of friends at the camp. There were the waitresses in the snack bar, the barmaids Sheila and Shirley, and of course Sid, a portrait painter and sketch artist, would draw the campers in crayon for five shillings. His portraits were so lifelike I asked him to draw one of me, to which he kindly obliged. I still have my portrait, and photos of some of the friends (especially Sheila and Shirley) that I met all those years ago, to this very day. I also kept a picture of my favourite friend Toni Manning, a pretty young woman of twenty-five. Being only thirteen, naturally I fell madly in love with her. Toni used to take me to the funfair, buy me sweets and generally keep an eye on me when she had time.

I went in for most of the competitions, including the 'Knobbly Knees', which I didn't win, but I did win the boy with the best physique contest, also a couple of table-tennis tournaments.

Most evenings I went dancing with Mum, but usually ended up having to go back to the chalet on my own, as she would be with the 'Orchestral Wives', gas-bagging at the bar! Still, I had made plenty of friends and learned to dance. During that holiday and on future ones at Butlin's, I met Peter Townshend,[1] son of Cliff, who had just joined the Squadronaires on second alto, and Tommy McQuater son of Tommy, who played in the BBC Show Band in later years amongst other Squadronaire Juniors.

Some days a few of us 'sprogs' would walk to Jaywick Sands and go for a swim. It was there I met Lottie once more.

Toni had walked with us to Jaywick but said that she would have to leave us, as she had to act as one of the judges in a 'Bathing Beauty Contest'. I said that I would be o.k. and would see her later.

I ran into the foamy sea and was splashing about and jumping over the waves when I accidentally bumped into someone.

"Whoops, sorry," I said apologetically, and as I turned around, I nearly fell flat on my face. There was Lottie, just as beautiful as when I had last seen her waving goodbye to me a year ago. She had matured dramatically and was a young woman now.

"Peter darling," she said, hugging and kissing me. I blushed, just as I had done when she had told me I had a beautiful voice. It seemed like a lifetime ago.

"It's wonderful to see you again, Lottie," I said.

We spent the rest of the day together, swimming, talking, and generally enjoying ourselves.

"Where are you staying, Lottie?" I asked her.

"I live here in Jaywick Sands with my Mum and Dad," she answered.

---

[1] Peter later achieved worldwide fame with rock group 'The Who'.

"I will be here for another six weeks," I told her.

"Oh, that's marvellous!" she said excitedly, "We will be able go see each other every day."

She seemed thrilled to be with me again.

"When will I see you again?" she asked me.

"Give me your phone number. I will ring you tomorrow," I said.

Lottie gave me her number and I went back to the camp for dinner.

When I returned to the chalet, Mum was waiting for me.

"Where have you been, Peter? she demanded.

"I have been to Jaywick Sands, swimming," I answered.

"Well, you might have told someone where you were going," she retorted angrily.

Poor old me! I never seemed to be able to do anything right.

"I went with Toni, but she had to come back to judge the Beauty Contest. Then I bumped into Lottie," I explained, feeling quite fed up with everything and everybody.

"Who is Lottie?" Mum asked.

So I told her how I had met Lottie at Auntie's, expressing my delight at seeing her once more, and the fact that she lived nearby at Jaywick. This seemed to pacify Mum.

"Give me the telephone number so that I can ring Lottie's parents, introduce myself and make arrangements to pick her up in the car, then we will all go horse-riding tomorrow. How does that strike you?"

I thought that was a marvellous idea. I knew Mum and Dad were good riders but I had never been. Mum, true to her word, rang Lottie's parents and made all the arrangements. I felt extremely happy and thanked her. She obviously was trying to make up for the years she had been apart from me.

The next morning Mum, Dad, Lottie and I went riding. We arrived at the stables at Jaywick at seven o'clock and met Florence Harris, an upright, grey-haired lady of some fifty years, red-faced and weather-beaten due to her outdoor life, but of a very kindly disposition.

"Hello there," she boomed (Lottie thought she had a voice like a 'Fog-Horn').

"Good-morning," we all replied at once.

"Have you ever sat a horse before?" she asked, looking at Lottie and me.

"No," we both answered.

"We'll soon put that right," Mrs. Harris told us.

My parents had their usual horses – 'Heidi', a grey mare for Mum, and 'Fritz', a German stallion for Dad. Lottie and I each had a pony. Lottie's pony went by the name of 'Mischief' and was true to her name, for instance, pinching Florence's hat from her head and running off with it. Florence saddled 'Blackie' for me to ride, he was black as night and his mood wasn't all that bright either.

"As long as you are firm with him," Florence told me, "He will behave. Be kind, but don't stand any nonsense!"

"Are we going to ride now? I asked.

"Oh no," she answered, "First of all we have to do the mucking out!"

"What's that?" Lottie asked, with a horrified look on her face.

"I will show you," Florence answered, "And from now on you can call me Flo."

Flo led us to the stalls, where the horses were 'bedded down'. We were greeted by a shocking smell – only natural, of course, but we would have to get used to it. Flo gave a rake to each of us, a bucket, soap and water, and lastly a scrubbing brush.

"It is the responsibility of each of us to clean out our horse's stall, so come on Lottie and Peter, I will show you what to do. First we rake out the old straw, then we clean out the stall with soap and water, adding a little disinfectant to kill the germs and make the stall smell more pleasant, if that is at all possible. Now let it dry, while we have a cup of tea, then afterwards make their beds with fresh straw."

We had tea and then resumed our tasks and Flo continued her demonstration.

"We rake the fresh straw around so that the horses and ponies will be nice and comfortable," she said, "and there you have it – the beds are made."

"That was good fun," Lottie and I chirped up together.

"Well… it is, unless you have to do it every day for twenty horses and ponies!" Flo explained, laughing.

"The only thing now is," Lottie said wearily, "I feel too tired to ride."

"You will be fine, once we get going," Flo assured her, "Now, 'to horse!' This is the most important part of the lesson, so listen carefully. First, we have to saddle the ponies, children" (Mum and Dad had been through that routine before, and were quite adept at it). Flo continued… "All the time that you are doing anything to your mount, you must comfort him and talk gently to him, stroke him, and then he will let you do virtually anything!"

Flo had to help us children to lift our saddles, as they were exceptionally heavy, "When the saddle is in place, the correct way around," she laughed, "We must tighten the girth. That is the strap that goes underneath the horse's belly, but not too tight as he must be able to breathe.

The next step is to mount. First face towards the hind-quarters of your pony, being careful not to get too near to his hind legs, just in case he lashes out at you. Next, take hold of the reins with your right hand, putting your foot in the stirrup twisting the strap first, throw your left leg over his haunches, then you are mounted."

That seemed 'just a piece of cake' to me, but proved not quite as easy as I thought. It took me a few attempts to get the hang of it, but Lottie had no trouble at all, she was a natural, just like my Mum and Dad. At last we were ready for the off, but Flo said, "Before we go, grip tightly with your knees, as this will leave your hands free to hold the reins with one hand, and do your signals with the other one."

With that, Flo took hold of Lottie's lead-rein, leaving Dad to take a grip on mine, and off we trotted.

What a beautiful day, the sun shining brightly, not too hot, with just a light breeze gently blowing the trees and making our faces tingle.

"All keep together!" Flo warned, "We are going to cross the main road."

We stopped at the kerb's edge, waited for traffic to pass, then we crossed. We rested for a half-hour, for Flo to show us how to ride 'At the trot'.

"As you may, or may not know," Flo began… "Horses generally prefer to trot, rather than walk, so we have to know how to ride 'at the trot', without making our bottoms sore, by bumping up and down in the saddle. Stand up in the stirrups, holding onto the reins tightly, then gently lower yourself into the saddle again. You may find this awkward at first, but as you get used it, this will come quite naturally."

As Flo had predicted, it took a few practices, but then came quite easily to them.

The group rode for an hour, then returned to the riding school. After warning us that they would be stiff in the morning Flo bade us farewell saying, "See you next week children."

With that, Mum, Dad and I took Lottie home and returned to the camp.

The next morning, as Flo had predicted, I woke up feeling as if my body did not belong to me. Everything hurt, my legs were stiff, bottom sore, and my arms would not function properly, I really thought that I had died! Mum laughed and said, "Flo did warn you that you would be stiff-jointed this morning, Peter."

"Yes I know," I replied, "But I did not expect to feel as if a steamroller had gone over me!" I had taken a bath the night before and my Mum had put some bath salts in it, but it did not appear to have had much effect. Perhaps a cold shower would do the trick? After the shower, I felt a little better and went with Mum to the dining-hall for breakfast. I enjoyed the meals there because, as everywhere else on the camp, I had made friends. I started my breakfast with a bowl of cornflakes, then another, and after that a third. Following that, two slices of toast and jam and two cups of tea. That was my usual breakfast.

My Dad had stayed in bed so Mum and I had gone to breakfast without him. We arrived back at the chalet to find that Dad had got out of bed and dressed ready to go out. He turned to me and said, "Where shall we go today? There is no tea dance again, due to renovations in the ballroom."

Mum suggested picking up Lottie then going to one of the bays for a picnic. We had found a pleasant spot, just the other side of Jaywick. Both Dad and I agreed, so we bought some sandwiches, cakes, and a flask of coffee from the café, then climbed into Cuvvie. We picked up Lottie on the way and were introduced to her parents. I thought they were rather pleasant.

"See you later," Lottie said to her Mum and Dad, then off we went. We found a scenic spot near to the beach with plenty of trees to shield us from the sun. Dad was a powerful swimmer, Mum couldn't swim a stroke and Lottie just a few strokes. As for me, though I hated to admit it, I felt afraid of the water. I could swim, of course, but due to an accident while living with Auntie, felt nervous about it... I had gone to the reservoir, quite a distance from Auntie's, with Lottie and another little boy. We had been playing ball, and when I missed a catch, it had fallen into the water. The reservoir did not seem very deep at the edge, but there was a warning sign whch read: 'DANGER, treacherous undercurrents, NO BATHING!' I had jumped backwards to catch the ball, but had overbalanced and had fallen into the water. When I tried to stand up, I found that I could not.

"Lottie, help me, I can't swim very well," I called, "Please get Sean."

It must have been two miles to Sean's house, but there was no need to look for him. There was a splash and there he was, pulling me to safety.

"Where on earth did you come from, Sean?" I asked, wringing the water out of my clothes.

"I called for you, then remembered that sometimes, we visited the old haunted house near the reservoir, and here I am," Sean replied, hugging me.

"Thank goodness for a friend like you, Sean!" I said, my heart pounding from such a frightening experience.

"We had better get home quickly, before we catch pneumonia," Sean said laughing...

I hadn't told my Mum and Dad about my experience in the reservoir. It had happened so long ago, but I did tell them now. We all went into the water together and with the help of my Dad, my confidence was soon restored.

It had been a wonderful day and, as all good things, quickly came to an end. Dad had to return to the camp to play for the evening dance.

I always looked forward to the latter part of the dance because at twelve o'clock there was a parade around the camp. It started with 'The Campers Song'...

Good night campers, I can see you yawning
Good night campers, see you in the morning
You must cheer up, 'cause you'll soon be dead
For I've heard it said, that folks die in bed.
So I 'll say,
Goodnight campers, don't sleep in your braces
Goodnight campers, soak your teeth in Jeye'ses
Drown your sorrow, bring the bottles back tomorrow
Good night campers, goodnight!

Lottie and I sang until our throats were dry, and then the parade began. The dance orchestra led the way, playing, 'Please put a Penny on the Drum', another singalong tune, but this time on the march...

Please put a penny on the drum, on the drum
Please put a penny on the drum, on the drum
We've only got a tanner,
To buy a new pian-er
So please put a penny on the drum.

Come and join us, come and join us
Come and join our happy party
Come and join us, come and join us
Come and join our happy band.

The procession marched through the camp until it reached the swimming pool, then the fun began. The 'Redcoats' had dressed up in clowns' costumes and as you may well imagine, were one by one, ducked in the swimming pool. The night (or should I say morning), ended with a sing-song, then it was time for bed. There were many nights like that for me, and it made me think that life wasn't so bad, after all.

But unfortunately the holiday was coming to an end and the time had come to say goodbye to Lottie once more.

On the last week of my holiday, the four of us went horse riding again, for the last time, and that nearly was the last thing I ever did! A bit of a stormy day, but nothing really to worry about, so as usual, Flo took us four riders out with her. We'd had quite a breathtaking gallop and were just trotting along when suddenly Blackie reared up onto his hind legs and threw me from his back. If only I could have stopped myself from rolling, I would have been quite safe, because Dad's horse, Fritz, would have jumped over me. Unluckily for me, I kept rolling over and over and Fritz's hoof caught me in the ribs, breaking two of them, another scar for me to carry for the rest of my life.

I spent two weeks in hospital and although the ribs healed quite quickly I had to be strapped up for weeks after that. Poor Flo, she blamed herself for what had happened, but we all told her not to be so silly. How could she be held responsible for what had been just an accident?

The last day of the holiday arrived and of course I became upset, to say the least. I said my goodbyes to everyone and a special one to Lottie, because I did not expect to see her ever again. At least I had my portrait and photographs of my friends to remind me of them and the most exciting holiday I had ever experienced (forgetting the accident of course!).

The drive home to London did not present any untoward incidents, except that we had to stop at one point due to Cuvvie's exhaust system going wrong and leaking fumes into the car. Luckily we found a garage nearby and Dad managed to get the problem fixed. The smell had upset me a little, but after a walk in the fresh air, I felt a little less queasy, enabling us to continue our journey home without further interruption.

The last few months at boarding school were not too bad, and after that, I would be spending the last of my schooldays at day school. I would have to travel to Harrow by bus every day, but I didn't mind, anything was better than Boarding School.

My piano playing advanced rapidly and I passed quite a lot of examinations. I used to enjoy playing duets with Mum, in fact the two of us became quite friendly, if not as close as one would expect mother and son to be. The draughts set came into play quite a lot and the two of us would sit for quite a while playing. I usually ended up winning, but Mum accused me of cheating. I didn't, of course, but I had to humour her!

Luckily I didn't have to suffer the bullying or any of the other problems that I had to put up with at boarding school, and I soon settled down at Chester College, Harrow. I attained reasonable results in my exams, but once more the only subjects I excelled in were French and Music. The headmaster, Mr Jackson, another strict disciplinarian, did not have any favourites like Mr Hodges, thank goodness.

'What a coincidence, Auntie's name is Jackson', I thought. There the similarity ended. Auntie was a kind and considerate person, but it takes all sorts to make a world. The two teachers I had to be wary of were Mr Foley and Mr Ferguson. Mr Foley the sports master, was an ex-professional footballer and on the sports field we had a lot of fun together, never shouting, but in the classroom… well that was a different story… he would not permit even the slightest indiscretion.

One day during a geography lesson, two of the pupils were talking when they were supposed to be paying attention when he threw a wooden ruler at them, hitting one of the boys. Another time, when I looked out of the window, Mr Foley crept up behind me and hit me around the head, causing me to go flying across the room. This may seem a bit drastic and cruel, but he did command respect!

Mr Ferguson had a bite worse than his bark, he sometimes used his fists – a typical bully – anger is one thing, but he could have injured one of us seriously. He taught maths and sometimes would fly into a terrible rage, especially if boys were looking out of the window at the girls passing by (not that I would, of course!).

Wednesday afternoon was the regular day for sports and physical training. One particular day the boys were playing a football match against a rival school. We were old adversaries, and at half time our teams were level at one goal each. During the interval we were all taking refreshments and having a friendly chat. Although deadly enemies on the pitch, we were all pals otherwise. One of the lads on the other team pulled out a packet of cigarettes and offered them around. Luckily, the teachers were in the school common room, having their tea. The boys, in turn, refused politely, but I would have to try one. If I had stopped to think I would have remembered my Great Uncle Walt and the cough he had due to smoking, but instead I lit the cigarette, inhaled the smoke, and nearly choked. All my friends laughed, but Stuart my best friend told them off, and then told me off for being so stupid!

"How are you going to play in the second half, Peter?" he asked.

"Not very well," I spluttered, rushing off to the toilet to be sick.

Somehow I managed to pull myself together and resumed the match with the others. After a dour struggle my team won 3 – 1. After the match, we had tea. What a spread! The parents had been invited also, and Tommy and Rachel had managed to be present, so that pleased me. I had made a vow never to smoke another cigarette, and kept it until I reached the age of fifteen.

Auntie Betsy had written her weekly letter to me, telling me that Uncle Walt would be coming to London for the FA Cup Final. It was, and still is, the most important event in the football calendar. Unfortunately Auntie would not be able to accompany him, due to her legs being troublesome and not allowing her to travel. Due to his position as Secretary of Bacup Borough Football and Cricket Club, Uncle had been able to obtain tickets for the Cup Final. It seemed strange to think that I lived within walking distance of Wembley Stadium but had to rely on my uncle to obtain tickets.

Uncle Walt arrived on the Friday evening before the match. My Mum and Dad met him at Victoria Coach Station. Uncle Walt really showed his pleasure at seeing me again. It had been such a long time.

"How's my Auntie?" I enquired.

"Nay too well, I'm feared Lad," Uncle answered, with a sad look on his face.

It gave me a thrill to hear that strong dialect once more, but it made me feel sad to hear of Auntie's ill-health.

"Is there nothing that can be done to cure her?" I asked.

"Did she tell you the story of how the accident happened?" Walt asked me.

"Yes Uncle," I replied. "She told me that when just a young woman she had been for a check up at the hospital soon after she had given birth to Ruth. She was holding the baby in her arms as she waited for a bus by the car park wall when a car parked in front of her shot forward. It had the old-fashioned starting handle sticking out of the front of the radiator and it pinned poor Auntie to the wall."

I could hardly carry on speaking, for the emotion I felt swelled up in my throat, choking me…

Uncle finished the tragic tale for me.

"Yes Lad, and the tragic part o' t'was that t'was 'er best friend and t'same surgeon, who 'ad delivered her baby, also a very dear friend. Luckily, instinct saved Ruth's life because, Auntie just threw your cousin onto t'grass bank, over t' wall. A terrible accident, no more. Apparently the car, instead of reversing, the gear lever accidentally slipped into first gear, and rolled forward instead. T'surgeon was so distraught, that he swore never to drive again, and he didn't to the best of my knowledge. The specialists said that Auntie would never again be able to walk, but Betsy is as stubborn a mule, and although she spent two years in hospital, having dozens of operations on her legs, she beat all the odds and walked again. She has lived in pain all these years, but never complains."

The next day was Saturday, so Uncle and I got up early, dressed, had our breakfast, then went to the West End of London for Uncle to see the sights, before we went to the football match.

"Where would you like to go first, Uncle?" I asked him.

"Let's go for a walk down Oxford Street," Walt answered, "then I c'n buy Auntie a present."

"Right Uncle," I agreed.

The only time that I went to the West End was to see Dad playing with the Squadronaires, so I found it quite exciting, even for me. We walked up and down Oxford Street, until we found the shop that Uncle wanted. He bought a scarf with the map of London on it, and a lovely brooch. Auntie always loved brooches. We went into Lyons' Corner House for a coffee, then went on to Trafalgar Square, stopping to admire Nelson's Column and feeding the pigeons. Uncle looked at his watch and said, "Hey yung 'un we'll 've t' get t' train f'r Wembley."

We went down the escalator at Oxford Circus Station, but what crowds confronted us! After waiting for half of an hour, we squeezed ourselves into a carriage and we were on our way to Wembley.

Two teams from the North of England were meeting in the final, so it didn't really matter to us who won, the competition being the most important thing. The match had everything that a final should have, and excited the pair of us. Uncle and I cheered ourselves hoarse, and finally, when the match ended, we walked home to Neasden. Uncle Walt would be going to make that journey to the Cup Final twice more, the next year and the year after that. I would have that to look forward to at least. Uncle stayed until Sunday evening, then he had to return to Bacup.

The time soon arrived for me to leave school, so my Dad asked me what I would like to do, as a career. The answer, pretty obvious I would have thought: to be a professional musician like him. Billy Matthews, a close friend of Dad's, a professional clarinettist and teacher, said that he would be only too pleased to teach me how to play the clarinet. It gave me quite a thrill to hear this news, that's what I really wanted. Unfortunately for me, I would only receive three lessons from my tutor before Billy died of a heart attack. Even so, the time I spent with him was invaluable. He instilled into me the importance of a perfect Clarinet tone. The days, weeks and months of 'Long Note Practise' (playing one note and holding it for a certain number of counts, then the same note for a longer number of counts, and so on). That procedure helped to produce a pure sound. That advice, amongst other excellent tips, helped me to become a very competent clarinettist in due course.

When practising, I used to alternate between the piano and the clarinet. The days were extremely long, travelling to school by bus, all day lessons, travelling home again, then at least two hours practise. Still, it did pay dividends, even though I never quite made it to the top of the professional ladder, like Dad.

Another important event had taken place in the Bradbury Family. I had acquired a sister. My Mum had given birth to a girl, weighing 10lbs, on 6th June 1949. At last, I thought, I would not be alone any more. What a beauty! (and still is, of course). She didn't have a lot of hair to begin with, but it was sandy coloured.

"Oh!" Rachel exclaimed, "I do hope that she is not going to be a 'Redhead."

Mum believed in the old-fashioned fallacy, about people with red hair having bad tempers.

"Stuff and nonsense," Dad retorted, "I reckon she will be a blonde."

"I think that she is beautiful anyway," I joined in.

We were all happy to welcome the newcomer. Our dog Lucky did not take the news too well though, he just sat in the corner, moping.

The next step in my training was clarinet lessons from Mr Goossens, the father of the famous Goossen family, but most people in the 'Musical Fraternity', called him Grandfather. I used to go to the Royal Academy of Music, Baker Street, London, once per week for lessons. I liked the old gentleman, and although stern he was an excellent teacher. By that time I had given up the piano lessons, but still kept up with my practising. I really did love my clarinet and would play it at every opportunity.

I had come to the end of my schooldays and had managed to fix myself up with a job. It wasn't much, but it enabled me to have a little pocket money and to give my Mother something for my keep. My first day at work was definitely something to be remembered (or to be forgotten, depending on how you look at it!).

The company, Smiths Jacking Systems, was a subsidiary of Smiths Clocks, situated at Cricklewood, on the Edgware Road, London, just fifteen minutes bus ride from Neasden. I took the No.16 bus outside our flat and had only two minutes walk at the other end. At 7am I knocked nervously on the door of the Foreman of the Stores, where I would be working. Mr Reid was a very stout, ferocious-looking man, but I would soon find out that if I performed my duties properly, that my boss had a very kind, understanding nature.

"Come in lad," Mr Reid shouted. I walked smartly into the small, dimly-lit office that smelled of grease and dirt.

"Just like home from home, eh lad?" Mr Reid said, laughing.

"Yes Sir," I answered.

My Boss picked up the internal phone.

"Nellie," he said, "Would you please come in here for a moment?" After a few moments an elderly woman came into the office, smiled and bade me "good morning."

"Pleased to meet you, Madam," I answered.

"I am Nellie," she informed me, "And I supervise the Stores where you are going to be working."

I thought that she looked rather nice, a bit like Auntie, in fact. "Come along Peter," Nellie said, leading the way to the Stores.

Even though my heart had been set upon becoming a musician, I would enjoy my short stay there. The Stores was an enormous place, but after a few weeks of Nellie 'showing me the ropes' I soon coped with everything quite easily. She showed me how to stock the shelves and told me what different things were used for.

The company manufactured industrial jacks, used for raising railway carriages and other heavy-duty vehicles. There were thousands of different nuts, bolts, and screws, plus many other engineering parts. My six months spent there were both interesting and educational. Every morning I had to take Lucky out for a walk, up at six, rush to Gladstone Park with the dog, dash back to the flat, then gulp down my breakfast and board the bus for work. I felt quite exhausted at the end of each day. By the time the weekend had arrived, I didn't feel like doing anything.

It seemed strange that Lottie had told me I should become a dancer. Even though I yearned to be a professional musician, I still had a special interest in dancing (probably due to Mum's career). I may have been worn out by the end of the week, but that did not stop me from going to the Wembley Town Hall (Later renamed the Brent Town Hall) most Saturday evenings, and using up all my energy jiving.

Whilst on the dance floor I wanted to be playing with the band, but on the occasions when I played, I wanted to be dancing – the obvious reason being that Mum had been a dancer and of course Dad a musician.

I met quite a lot of people when I went dancing and made many new friends. Even so, I did not neglect my clarinet practise. Nobody needed to prompt me because my mind had been made up to become a professional musician.

Although my favourite kind of music has always been big band jazz I had become an accomplished orchestral clarinettist and had joined the Edgware Symphony Orchestra, known to be one of the better amateur orchestras in London. I went to rehearsal every Tuesday evening. One of my favourite tunes was the New World Symphony, by Dvorak.

The new arrival had been named Christine and she showed our family that she possessed a strong pair of lungs. She had the bad habit of waking up two or three times during the night, which did not suit me one little bit. I also had to do my share of babysitting, which didn't please me either. I would not have minded too much, but I had so much to do in the evenings. Still, she would not be a baby forever. As well as taking Lucky out for a walk, I had to take my sister in the pram. A little embarrassing I must admit, but it did give me a chance to get some fresh air into my lungs, and meet my friends.

My grandmother and grandfather lived in Morden, Surrey, along with Uncle Jim. They had a beautiful semi-detached house with an enormous garden, in which they grew their own vegetables. Mum, Dad, Christine and I used to visit them once a month. My grandparents were both retired and Uncle Jim toured the world, playing with a band on the 'Coronia' cruise ship. Unlike his brother Tommy, Jim was not so proficient as a performer, more the theoretical genius of the two. I only saw my Uncle once during my childhood, and once when in my early twenties. Jim had been married, but was now divorced, so lived with his parents. The top floor of the house had been converted into a self-contained flat, so that he could have some privacy. His job kept him away for months on end, travelling on the ship on world cruises. I thought that would be an ideal life for me!

I liked to go with my grandparents for walks in the nearby woods. I got a thrill out of collecting the different types of leaves that were lying on the ground in autumn. I pasted them into a scrapbook, and eventually gathered quite a large collection. My grandparents were very keen on horse racing, taking me with them occasionally. The only problem with that being, I was not very tall. My Granddad had to lift me onto his shoulders, so that I could see the races (even at the age of fifteen I had not grown much, being only slightly built).

I found the horse racing really exciting. Granddad put one or two bets on for me. Naturally I did not win anything, I didn't expect to because I never had been a lucky boy. Grandma had all the luck. She used to bet on 'The Tote', which usually turned out to be more rewarding than using the 'Bookies'. Mind you, that has always been a bone of contention in betting circles. The 'Tick-Tack' men made me laugh, waving their arms about and signalling the betting odds to their colleagues at the other side of the racecourse.

They wore white gloves, but as they all were wearing them, it puzzled me. How on earth did each bookie recognise his own tick-tack man? I wondered.

At that time, I still saw a lot of Mum, as she had given up her dancing career, mainly due to me going to day school, another reason being that Dad did not tour around quite so often. By 1950 the 'Squadronaires Dance Orchestra had disbanded. Tommy Bradbury had joined the 'Eric Robinson Organisation', some of the musicians formed the 'BBC Show Band, and a small group calling themselves the 'Squad-cats', played on the radio, and did so until the early 1970s. I went with my Dad quite often to rehearsals and live shows at the television studios. The more I went, the more I longed to be a professional musician. I still made progress with my clarinet, but did become rather impatient. One evening, I visited the local pub, the 'Spotted Dog'. It made a pleasant change for us all to have a night out together. My Mum had asked Mrs Taylor our housekeeper, to babysit Christine, to give me a break.

My Dad introduced me to a friend of his, Curt Lang. He had his own engineering business at Cricklewood, NW London, not too far from Neasden. Curt came from Sweden, my parents having made friends with him while they lived there. He was a very influential person, but unfortunately for me, not in the world of music. Mr. Lang offered me a clerical job with his company and yet again Mum and Dad encouraged me to accept the offer. It seemed to me that my parents did not want me to become a musician.

I said goodbye to the friends I had made at Smiths' and although it made me feel sad to leave, I did not want to get into a rut. I started work at Clang's Electrical, but it wasn't very interesting, I endured it until I reached sixteen. I had been to visit my Auntie, Uncle and Ruth, but could not see them as often as I would have liked, due to the distance separating us.

In 1951 Uncle Walt came to London again for the FA Cup Final. The Festival of Britain also being celebrated that year. Uncle spent a whole week with us during the festivities and I had been given the week off from work as part of my holiday entitlement. This enabled us to spend some quality time together. Another big event of that year was the opening of 'Battersea Park Funfair'. Another was the introduction of the 'Festival Hall'. Both were situated on the Thames Embankment. Uncle bought a penknife, with the emblem representing the occasion on it for me, that I have kept to this day. We went for a boat trip up and down the Thames and had a drink together during the voyage. I downed a brown ale, my first real alcoholic drink, and smoked one of my Uncle's Capstan Full Strength cigarettes. Unfortunately I had forgotten my vow never to smoke again. Both my Mum and Dad smoked, Mum only about five per day, but Dad puffed away like a chimney.

Uncle's last visit to London was in 1952, the year Her Majesty Queen Elizabeth came to the throne. It did seem as if he thought he would never see me again, but he did just the once. One of the places we visited was the 'Houses of Parliament' in Westminster. Uncle could only spend three days with us on that occasion, and when the time came to return home to Lancashire, he cried! I had never seen Uncle cry before, not even when we had discussed Auntie's accident.

During that visit we played snooker together in the hall above Burtons the Tailors, at Neasden. We had only played a few frames when one of the local lads, who fancied his chances with the snooker cue, approached Walt and asked him for a game. The lad was not on his own. As usual, there were always one or two other youths hovering around. Uncle had become wise to snooker-hall 'hustlers' up North. Their ploy was to have a few frames for a couple of shillings, losing on purpose, then offering to play a further frame, doubling the stakes, only to lose again. Finally, after their opponents had been convinced they were only average players, the stakes would be raised again, then they would clean the 'mugs' off the table. But the hustlers had chosen the wrong person when picking on Uncle Walt. He played them at their own game and took their money.

'Perhaps I have taught those lads a lesson,' he said.

I don't think he had, though!

From the age of sixteen until seventeen I continued my musical studies at the London College of Music. I carried on playing my two favourite instruments, clarinet and piano. I had at last found a job associated with music, in Tin Pan Alley, one of the most famous streets in the world, and the heart of the music publishing business in London. I started work as a 'runner' for Peter Maurice Publishing, taking song-sheets and musical arrangements to other music wholesalers and suppliers in the West End and City of London. I also helped out in the packing department and could, if I had wished, have made a career out of music publishing.

If I had thought more about it, I might have gone into publishing more thoroughly, as it was the closest occupation associated with music I had found. But it wasn't to be, the only thing I wanted to do was perform my music in public.

On my travels between the publishers, I used to collect and deliver music for Frances' Music Supply, a shop situated at the junction of Tottenham Court Road and Charing Cross Road. The business was owned by father and son Harry (Pop) Frances and Derek. Derek offered me a job, which I readily accepted. They treated me very well, and although I found the work tiring, especially on my feet, I loved being out in the fresh air for most of the time, which certainly did me good! My actual job description was 'runner' (no comparison with a bookie's runner). A better description would be 'messenger boy'. I had to travel to work by 'tube', and although I didn't have to be there until eight-thirty, with one hour travelling, it certainly did make the day long.

As soon as I arrived at work I would make a pot of tea, using an old kettle I thought would have been better placed in a museum! It did serve the purpose, though. The one thing I hated the most was the journey in the tube. There were so many people commuting that we were all squashed like sardines. The caption on the side of the carriage that I travelled in one day, made me laugh. I saw an illustration of a group of 'sardines' standing up in a railway carriage, squashed together with the tin being opened by a key. The caption read: 'Don't be like Sardines – Avoid the Rush-Hour!'

I tried to board a non-smoking carriage as often as I could, but more often than not the crowd pushed me into a 'smoker'. Inevitably, there would be a pipe smoker in front of me, the thick smoke blowing into my face and choking me was disgusting, but with the thought of my musical future ahead, I felt that I could put up with anything!

One of the famous people I met from time to time was 'Piano Joe Henderson', then the boyfriend of Petula Clark and based at Peter Maurice Music Publishers, Tin Pan Alley, where I worked for a short while. I explained to Joe my dream of becoming a professional musician. As others before him, Joe encouraged me to keep on practising, then I would make the grade! John, the other 'runner' at Frances' Music Supply, was a very likeable person who treated me with kindness, and I got along with him extremely well. One day Derek drew me to one side, saying, "Peter lad, don't take what I am going to tell you too much to heart, but John is a pleasant person, though a bit weird, to say the least."

I smiled and said, "Yes Derek, he does say some peculiar things and act a bit strangely sometimes, but I just laugh at him and pass it off as 'just his way'."

"That is extremely generous of you lad, but you are a bit too young to understand fully," Derek replied.

"Try me," I urged.

"John is gay," Derek continued, "and so are plenty of the other runners." I had heard about such people before, but had not given the subject much thought. "Just laugh at John," Derek went on, "He won't bother you, nor will the others that you will be meeting."

"OK, I will," I said, "and thank you for warning me."

"It's my duty," Derek replied.

It's true to say that I did meet many 'gays' during my stay at Frances', but I found them quite amusing. One of them, Cyril, must have thought of himself a gipsy or pirate, because he wore one earring and a headscarf. I remained at Frances' until I reached the age of seventeen and a half, when the time came for me to join the Armed Forces. Actually, the conscription age at that time was eighteen, but I wanted to go into the Music Services, so I would have to sign up for five years, as a regular. Still, quite a lot would be happening before then...

One day, during the summer of 1952, while I still worked at Frances', I browsed through some travel brochures and an advert for holidays in Jersey caught my eye.

'Mmm...' I thought, 'I would like to go there'.

I asked Mum and Dad to go with me but they declined.

"Why don't you go on your own Peter?" Dad asked me.

"Yes dear," my Mum joined in, "You are old enough."

'Anyway', I thought, 'I am used to going places on my own', so I agreed with them.

I wrote off to the 'Merton Hotel' at St Helier, which in later years became better known as the 'Honeymoon Hotel', due to competitions in the national newspapers for newlyweds, with a first prize being a fortnight's holiday at the Merton Hotel, Jersey. I booked up for two weeks, and early one morning my Dad drove me to Heathrow Airport.

Off I went to enjoy my holiday, leaving my clarinet behind, although on arrival at the island, I wished I had not done so. It took only one hour to fly to St Helier airport and the journey, though pleasant, was uneventful. Snacks were served on the plane but I felt too excited to bother about eating or drinking. After disembarking I had to go through customs, then hailed a taxi. The day turned out to be one of the hottest on record, and I felt quite relieved when we reached the hotel. I paid off the taxi and climbed the steps to the entrance of the hotel. The commissionaire touched the peak of his cap, bidding me a 'good morning'.

"Hello," I replied, and proceeded into the foyer.

I booked in and the bell-boy showed me to my room. It faced the sea and the view could not have been more beautiful. As usual, I had been given room number six. Strange as it may seem, everywhere I went the number 6 seemed to be prominent. My room at boarding school had been number 6, the flat at Neasden, the same, then, to top it all, the no.16 stopped outside our block of flats. Maybe 6 could be my lucky number, but what luck? I had never been lucky, but perhaps that would all change one day...

I couldn't have picked a better time of year to have my holiday in Jersey. The 'Battle of Flowers' took place during the second week. If anyone had not witnessed this event, they really have missed something! I unpacked my case, had a shower and went down to the dining hall. The room was spacious and there were many waiters and waitresses. They reminded me of a crowd of penguins, in their black and white uniforms, hustling backwards and forwards. A pretty blonde girl by the name of Sheila showed me to my table.

Although she looked nothing like my friend at Butlins, she had the same pleasant nature. I would be seeing quite a lot of Sheila during the following two weeks. I imagine that she would be about the same age as me, sixteen or seventeen maybe. Anyway, I had gone on holiday to enjoy myself, and I would do just that! The meal tasted wonderful, smoked salmon for a starter with soup to follow, my favourite, mushroom, with a brown crusty roll smothered with butter. A choice of meat followed: steak, pork, or veal cutlets. I settled for the pork chop, naturally! Roast potatoes, garden peas and mushrooms were served up with the meat. Following that, a fruit sundae, then cheese and biscuits and coffee to round off the meal. I consumed a couple of glasses of white wine with the main meal, so by the time I had finished, I felt quite drowsy.

After dinner, I changed into my swimming costume, went down to the beach and fell asleep. When I awakened, I could hear someone shouting in French. I had learned enough at school to understand that the young girl whom was speaking felt distressed. She was crying and telling an elderly couple that someone had stolen her purse. That was the beginning of a new relationship for me.

I opened my eyes, 'Gosh, what a beautiful girl!' I thought, "Can I help?" I asked.

"I don't know," she replied, "But thank you for asking."

I felt relieved, because although I speak French fairly fluently, I didn't fancy having to speak the language for too long.

"You speak English perfectly," I said to her.

"Actually, I am English," she answered, "It is my Father who is French.

Regina le Geyt was born in England, daughter of an English mother and French father. Her father, a rich hotelier and a 'tax-exile' had moved to Jersey when Regina was very young. She was the same age as me, sixteen and a half. She had short curly hair, hazel eyes, a beautiful little snub-nose and a lovely mouth. How could I help her to find the purse? Suddenly, a scuffle broke out a few yards from us.

There were two policemen in uniform and a man with a woman arguing, in English. Apparently, the woman, a plain-clothes detective posing as a holidaymaker, had caught the thief red-handed, trying to steal her handbag. Regina, the elderly couple and I hurried to the spot to see what the commotion had been about.

"Is this your purse?" one of the officers asked Regina.

"Yes it is," she answered, breathing a sigh of relief.

"I'm afraid that I will have to ask you to come along to the police station," the woman detective said, apologetically, then went on, "We will need a statement from you. We won't be able to return your purse until after the trial, due to the fact that it will have to be used in evidence."

"I understand," Regina said, "But I haven't any money to get home."

"Don't worry," I offered, "I will take you home."

"That's extremely kind of you," she answered, "I don't live all that far, but it is a fair bus ride to Grave de Lec."

"I will pay," I offered.

"First of all, we will have to go to the police station," Regina said, not wanting the day to end, as she had found a new friend!

We went with the officers and Regina gave her statement, then I took her home.

The le Geyts lived in a most unusual mansion, shaped like a giant horseshoe, the reason being that her family were keen horse people. As I had become quite proficient at the sport prior to my accident, I found myself readily accepted at the le Geyt residence. Regina's mother and father were really impressed with me, although I can't for the life of me think why, and thanked me for being so kind to their daughter.

"Anything that you wish for, just ask, mon ami," her Father said.

"Nothing thank you," I answered, "It has been my pleasure."

After a splendid meal with Lottie's family and spending the evening at Monsieur le Geyt's club, the chauffeur drove me back to the Merton Hotel in the Rolls Royce. It really had been an exhausting beginning to my holiday and I felt tired. I went to bed at 1am and slept like a log.

At seven o'clock the same morning, I felt a hand on my shoulder.

"Good morning, Sir." Sheila stood there holding a cup of tea in her hand. I felt a little embarrassed at being caught in my pyjamas by a beautiful girl in my bedroom.

"Hello Sheila," I replied, "And don't call me sir, my name is Peter.

She giggled at the sight of me, holding the bedclothes up to my chest.

"That's a nice name," she said, "Extremely manly sounding!"

"Thank you for the compliment," I said, blushing.

"You are shy though, aren't you?" Sheila remarked.

"Yes, I'm afraid that I am, a little," I answered.

"See you at breakfast then," she said finally, tossing her hair backwards and forwards in a teasing manner and wiggled out of the room.

'Good heavens!' I thought, 'I seem to be surrounded by beautiful girls'. I jumped out of bed, had a shower, shaved, and went down to the dining hall for breakfast. My old habit of eating three bowls of cornflakes, two slices of toast with jam, and coffee hadn't altered. Sheila saw to it that I continued to have just that.

I had arranged to meet Regina on the beach at ten o'clock, but Sheila had caused me a problem by asking me to go out with her. She had the day off and had booked on a coach trip to Corbiere, to visit the famous lighthouse there. I could see that I would have to be tactful. I offered her my apologies, explaining about Regina and myself. Sheila appeared disappointed but said, "That's alright Peter, perhaps another time."

"Yes Sheila," I answered, "But thanks for asking."

I didn't want to have any problems during my holiday, but at the same time, didn't want to hurt either of their feelings.

Things worked out just fine though, due the fact that I couldn't see Regina every day, and Sheila worked shifts. I took them out alternately, and as each one knew about the other, everything turned out perfectly.

When I arrived at the beach I found Regina waiting for me. She greeted me with a hug and a kiss. For some peculiar reason, as soon as she did that, I thought of Lottie. We spent the whole day together, swimming, riding on the donkeys, and generally enjoying ourselves. I bought some postcards with views of the local places of interest, then sat down on the sand and wrote them out: one to Auntie, Uncle and Ruth, one to Lottie, and one to Mum, Dad and Christine.

Every evening I went dancing. One night I went to the West Park Pavilion at St Helier, then to the hotel ballroom on another. One particular evening, Regina had gone visiting with her parents, and Sheila had to go on duty. That left me to go dancing by myself, at the hotel ballroom. I spruced myself up, putting on me evening dress suit, complete with dickie-bow, then polished my shoes until I could see my reflection in them. With my heavy suntan I looked quite handsome and mature for my sixteen and a half years. I walked into one of the hotel bars and ordered my favourite drink – 'John Collins'. The drinks in Jersey were ridiculously cheap in those days, only two shillings for a 'John Collins'. The recipe for the drink: dip the rim of a tumbler in sugar, using one measure of gin, one tiny drop of Angostura Bitters, top up the glass with lemonade, then add a slice of lemon and ice cubes. It really is a refreshing drink, and I became quite fond of it. I shouldn't really have been drinking alcohol, but I was on holiday after all, and normally would very rarely indulge. As I sat at the bar chatting to Claude, the French barman, two girls came in and sat alongside me. "Deux John Collins, s'il vous plait," said the elder of the two girls, who were obviously French.

"Oui certainment, Madamoiselle," Claude answered.

The younger girl looked at me.

"Excuse my friend," she said, smiling, "She is French, you know."

"I did realise that," I replied, looking at her in admiration.

"What's your name?" she asked.

'This girl is a bit forward', I thought, but politely told her my name. 'Oh dear,' I mused to myself, 'Here we go again. There is certainly no shortage of girls here,' then turned to them and said,

"Shall we take our drinks into the ballroom?"

"Yes let's," they both replied.

I spent the whole evening with Georgette and Mary, finding them excellent company.

A sextet were playing for the dancing: piano, string-bass, drums, guitar, trumpet, with alto saxophone doubling on clarinet. The popular songs of that era were 'Somewhere Along the Way', 'On the Street where you Live', 'I Talk to the Trees' and many others. I had become quite partial to these three tunes. Later that evening, during the interval, I had a chat with the saxophonist whom, when he found out that I played the clarinet, suggested that I should sit in with the band for a couple of numbers.

"I haven't brought my clarinet with me," I explained.

"That's alright," the musician said, "You may borrow mine."

I was thrilled and accepted the offer.

The bandleader announced that the time had come for some 'Dixieland' tunes, my cue to sit in with the band. The two girls were impressed, even though they had been deprived of a dancing partner, they thoroughly enjoyed jiving to the Dixieland music. It certainly had been an exciting evening and at the end of it, Frank the saxophonist suggested that I should sit in with them again, another evening. In fact, I could, if I wished, join in with them anytime. I said that I would love to, and thanked Frank.

I said goodnight to the girls, then went to bed.

The end of the holiday all too soon approached and I would have to take my leave of sunny Jersey, but before that the climax to my holiday had been reached. 'The Battle of Flowers' brought the whole island out onto the streets. I got up early, breakfasted, then made my way to the start of the parade. Regina and Sheila were both there to greet me, which pleased me, as they had made my holiday at Jersey a happy one. I would be sad to leave Jersey, but all good things had to come to an end, eventually.

The floats were beautiful but the musical display impressed me the most. The lads from the hotel band had arranged the most original float in the parade, though admittedly one would have to be a musician to fully appreciate it. Basically it was a musical 'stave' made from wire. It consisted of a frame with five horizontal lines, one above the other with a space between each one, to represent the stave. The crotchets and quavers were suspended by wires from the stave and the lines were covered in white carnations, red and white roses, plus a variation of different coloured flowers. The musicians wore black jackets with white trousers, and straw hats to put the finishing touch to a brilliant display. Inevitably, their float won the First Prize.

Finally, after the parade had come to its conclusion and the judging was finished, the flowers were used by everyone to pelt each other with, hence the name 'Battle of Flowers'. It did seem such a pity to destroy all those beautiful floats, but that's tradition for you!

I spent my last evening in Jersey dancing with Regina. Sheila had already bid me a fond farewell at the dinner table. She had to return home, as her Mother had been taken ill. We went to the West Park Pavilion, and later after the dance finished, we went swimming together for the last time. Afterwards, I took Regina home and felt quite sorry to have to say goodbye to her. I promised to write to Regina and her parents, then went back to the hotel.

The following day I said farewell to the sunny island of Jersey. My Mum and Dad met me at Heathrow Airport and it was late afternoon by the time that we arrived at the flat. I had plenty of time to unpack and have a rest, ready for work the next day.

My lifestyle would soon change. I worked at Frances' Music Supply until May 1953, when I joined the Royal Air Force, and at the suggestion of my parents, went into the 'Music Services'.

Ann, Jenny and the Author, outside the Merton Hotel, Jersey.

Sheila and Shirley at Butlin's, Clacton.

Lottie and the Author, dancing at the Merton Hotel, Jersey.

Toni Manning, the Redcoat at Butlin's, Clacton.

Regina Le Geyt at the Merton Hotel, Jersey.

3.   The Royal Air Force

Conscription still existed in 1953 and as I was now seventeen and a half years of age, I would soon be called up. My Dad had a chat with me, about joining the RAF.

"As soon as you are eighteen you will have to serve two years in one of the three services," he said to me.

"Yes I know," I answered.

"Why don't you join the Royal Air Force and sign on for five years, to enable you to continue your musical career?" Dad suggested, then continued "I enjoyed my time in the Central Band, and even more so in the Squadronaires."

"I don't really relish the thought of staying in the forces for five years, Dad," I answered him.

"Isn't it better than being forced into something, you won't enjoy for two years?" Dad asked.

"Yes, I suppose so," I retorted, a bit sceptically.

"Well son, it's up to you," Dad concluded.

In April of that year, I went to the Recruitment Centre at Kingsway, Holborn, and signed on. One week later, I received my orders, to report to Cardington for Kitting Out, and to be sworn in. I was accustomed to being away from home, so being in the Forces, wouldn't worry me at all, though the thought of having to spend five years in uniform, wasn't too encouraging. It did seem like a long while, but time alone would tell. I almost had second thoughts about signing on for five years, but as I would be able to play my music for most of the duration, I signed on as a regular airman.

On May 5th 1953 Peter Bradbury became 4128164, Aircraftman Bradbury, Peter. I had to be stationed at RAF Cardington for one week. Even though I had been away from home many times before, this experience had a different feel. There were twenty five entrants in my group. They came from every walk of life. There were bank clerks, mechanics, medical students, and even a farmer. I was the only one of that group to enlist in the music services. The young men were allowed three days in which to change their minds before taking the oath of allegiance. Some of them were conscripts, called up at the age of eighteen to serve two years National Service. Some of the others wished to extend their contracts to three years Regular Service. The remainder, including myself, wished to specialise in the career of our choice, and had no option but to sign on for five years.

The sergeant and corporal in charge of our intake were both kind and helpful to us lads. Most of the recruits were far away from home for the first time and until they had officially committed themselves they could change their minds and transfer into one of the other two branches of the armed forces. We spent the first couple of days collecting our bedding, being kitted out with uniforms, and generally becoming accustomed to service life. The beds weren't particularly comfortable, having iron frames with really rough blankets. The sheets were starched, making them quite stiff. The food wasn't too bad, I suppose, not exactly what one would be served with at the Ritz, but edible! The hardest thing to get used to was having to get up at 5.30 each morning. The corporal entered the billet each day and bellowed, "Wakey, wakey! Rise and shine lads!"

It amused me greatly to see the different reactions to that rude awakening. Some of the lads nearly jumped through the roof while others just turned over in their beds, but were promptly turfed out of them.

After washing, shaving and getting dressed, the airmen were lined up and marched in formation to the mess. After breakfast we were marched back again to the billet by the sergeant and corporal shouting, "Left, right, left, right, left... Smarten up there! Keep in line! You are not supposed to enjoy yourselves! What a scruffy shower you are!"

The Kitting Out gave me the biggest laugh of that first week. My blue uniform must have been made for someone twice my size. The trousers dragged on the floor and the sleeves of the jacket covered my hands. Thank goodness the Camp Tailor could alter them for me. The material of the uniform appeared to be thick and none too comfortable, but after being tailored it looked reasonably smart.

As well as the uniform we lads were issued with two pairs of vests, pants, socks, physical training shorts, plimsolls, and virtually everything that we would need during our term of service. Our rifle and combat equipment were to be issued at Training Camp, at a later date.

We kept the camp barber extremely busy during that first week, the order of the day being 'short back and sides'. I had fairly long hair, at least for that era, and after my visit to the barber I felt as though I had been scalped.

Finally, came the 'Swearing In', the point of no return for us young men. Once we had been sworn in, there would be no turning back. Quite an ordeal really! One by one the men were marched in before the Commanding Officer by the sergeant and corporal. The 'oath' was not too lengthy but to me it seemed like an eternity as I made my promise 'to serve God and the Queen...'

On the last day of my stay at RAF Cardington the sergeant and corporal came into the billet to give us our orders for the following week. We lads were given leave passes and a railway warrant each, for free travel to our homes. I had been allowed one week off to prepare myself for eight weeks basic training at West Kirby, Wirral, Cheshire, which was the camp I would be going to. That evening, being Saturday, the sergeant and corporal joined us men for a drink in the NAAFI canteen. That concluded my first week in the RAF.

On Sunday morning, the airmen were able to lie in until eight o'clock. We went to the mess for the last time before leaving for our individual destinations. After that, the bedding had to be handed in to the clothing store, the billet cleaned out, then we were on our way home. I arrived home at teatime, and after eating, had plenty to tell my Mum and Dad. During my leave I wrote to Auntie, Uncle and Ruth. I related my experiences to them and said that I would be going to see them after my eight weeks of Basic Training.

The week passed by quickly and before I could say 'Spitfire' I had arrived at West Kirby.

RAF West Kirby was situated in open countryside and felt like the coldest place I had experienced outside Bacup. It seemed to me that my life had been moving round in circles. I had started off in Weymouth, moved to Sweden, then to London, on again to Lancashire, and back again to London. Off again to Cardington, yet again to London, and now to Cheshire.

Training Camp would make a long-lasting impression on me. I arrived towards the end of May 1953 and would be spending the most harrowing eight weeks of my life there. The nickname given to Basic Training is 'Square-bashing', and after spending so much of the eight weeks on the parade 'square', I can see the reason why. The drill instructors, again a sergeant and corporal, were entirely different in manner to the previous two. They had a special job to do: to turn civilians into airmen, and the only way to do that was to be tough themselves. The number one DI was Sergeant Drummond, nicknamed 'Bulldog' – and his nature matched the name. Both he and the Corporal DI met the Intake at the

Guardroom. The Corporal's name was Dent and he went by nickname of 'Basher'. It seemed that everything and everyone in the RAF had a nickname.

We airmen were taken to our billet, given a 'bed-space', then on to the 'Clothing Stores' to pick up our bedding. When one considers that twenty-six strangers were thrown together in a claustrophobic environment, it is amazing how well they could get along. That applied particularly to the forces, where we were 'all in the same boat'. One couldn't avoid the occasionally fight, but generally, we all got on well together.

The first Monday saw the New Recruits awakened at five-thirty by the bellowing of 'Bulldog' and 'Basher'. These guys really meant it! Not just a bit of fun, unlike Cardington. Woe betide anyone who did not get up immediately, they would be physically extracted from their beds by the NCOs, upending them. I recall only one person received this harsh treatment, his name was Derek, and he always got into trouble!

Everyone hated Training Camp, but accepted it as being necessary. Derek, on the other hand, made it painfully obvious that he would rebel at every command given him. The problem was that everyone else had to pay the penalty for his defiance.

The second shock of that first day occurred when we went to the 'ablutions'. A lack of hot water. Washing in freezing cold water seemed bad enough, but having to shave in it, was awful! I managed to shave eventually, but cut myself quite badly. It amused me though, to see some of the men on parade, with faces covered in plasters. Before breakfast, the billet had to be swept out, the floor polished and sheets folded at the head of the bed. Each blanket and sheet had to be an exact length, one matching the other. They were then laid alternately, one on top of the other, blanket, sheet, blanket and so on. Finally, the remaining blanket had to be wrapped around those. That had to be done every day. Virtually everything we airmen did was called a 'parade'.

Bulldog and Basher inspected the billet then called together, "Outside on Parade!" The men lined up outside the billet in two parallel lines.

"Atten...tion! By the right... dress!" Basher bellowed.

With that each man stood to attention, with feet together. He looked to his right, stretched out his right arm and touched the other man's left shoulder. This manoeuvre had to be repeated until each man stood level with the man on his right hand side. The men shuffled their feet, enabling them to perfect the drill. After ten minutes of bawling, Basher had formed the men into a reasonable line.

"Eyes front!" he shouted, and at the same time as obeying the command, we all brought our arms smartly to our sides.

"Into line, ri...ight, turn!" Basher continued then, "Dressing by the right, qu...ick march – left, right, left, right,, left..."

On arrival at the mess we found a long queue in front of us, so we would have to wait a long time for something to eat. We had been issued with our own knives, forks, spoons, two tin plates and a tin mug each. The cookhouse – enormous is an understatement – seated one thousand people. The food, although there was plenty of it, tasted disgusting. I queued up with the others and eventually, my turn came to be served. After cornflakes with watered down milk, greasy egg and bacon, bread with margarine (ugh!) and a mug of sweet tea with tinned milk in it, we had to wash up our own plates and cutlery. After breakfast, we were lined up again and marched back to the billet.

The floor shone like a new pin. Each bed-space was neat and tidy, with the blankets made up. The billet looked more like a ballroom with beds in it than living quarters. The first job was to get ready for 'Officer's Billet Inspection', before Marching Drill Parade.

"Stand by your beds!" Basher shouted. "Officer's Inspection at 0730 and woe betide anyone that the CO finds fault with!"

Flight Lieutenant Burke was the Unit Commanding Officer (one can imagine the nickname he acquired) and finnicky as a matron in a hospital. After all the hard work that my fellow airmen and I had put in, to make the billet spick and span, F/Lt Burke walked around each bed-space, wet his finger, then ran it along the top of each man's locker.

"Put all the men in this billet on fatigues, Sergeant," the officer said, "Dirty lockers!"

"Yes, Sir!" Bulldog snapped. "Corporal!"

Basher jumped to attention.

"Yes, Sergeant!" he replied, then turning to us, "You miserable misfits. It's fatigues for everybody, and you'll soon find out what that means."

'This is a funny way to gain respect', I thought, 'Still, I suppose they know what they are doing...'

After securing our lockers we lined up outside for marching drill. It would be our first taste of 'square-bashing'. The uniform: battledress with webbing belt, gaiters, beret and highly polished boots. We were brought up to attention, by Basher. After that, Bulldog inspected us. When he arrived at spot where Derek stood, he stopped and glared at him.

"What a disgusting excuse, for an airman!" the Sergeant said, turning to Basher. "Corporal, this man needs a haircut, his uniform needs pressing and his boots are dirty. Put him on a charge."

"Yes Sergeant," Basher answered, "Certainly Sergeant."

Bulldog, as he insulted Derek, had deliberately trodden on his boots, marking the shiny toecaps. I looked out of the corner of my eye at all that occurred.

'Thank goodness,' I thought, 'Derek is taking all the abuse without saying anything'.

Suddenly, without any warning, Derek brought up his knee, catching the Sergeant with full force in the groin, and ran. Although the men were amused by what had happened, we did not even dare to smile, just remained standing there, stiffly to attention. Basher ran after Derek, blowing his whistle. Two Service Police corporals appeared, as if from nowhere, then gave chase. They must have caught him, because Basher returned on his own, looking ruffled and angry. By this time Bulldog had recovered from his ordeal, then gave everyone a lecture on discipline.

"Parade, atten…tion," Basher snapped, "We are now going to have, two hours continuous 'square-bashing. I will make men of you yet."

Bulldog took over the commands shouting, "Into line, le…ft turn!" He then continued, "By the right in two's, quick march, left, right, left, right, left… Hey there Bradders, don't you know your left foot, from your right?" Poor me, I had started off on the wrong foot, in more ways than one.

When we arrived at the 'square', Bulldog yelled, "Squa…d, halt!" I did it again, falling over the man in front of me, making yet another mistake.

"Into line, righ…t turn," Bulldog continued, then, "Stand at ease, stand easy."

Bulldog headed straight for me, but instead of yelling at me, this time the Sergeant said, "I know this is your first day Bradbury, but please try to keep your ears open, they are for listening with, not for hanging your beret on!"

The DI's were generally full of surprises, but as promised the drill did last for two hours. Finally the airmen were given a break, in which to go to the NAAFI.

After a thirty-minute rest, Basher marched the 'Flight' to the Armoury where we collected our rifles and combat kit.

Finally, there came a most welcome break, for one hour and a half. Bulldog and Basher, had a short chat with the recruits, unofficially, before lunch. The topic of the discussion was Derek! I put a question to the NCO first.

"Please, Sergeant, what has happened to Derek?"

Bulldog remained silent for a moment, before answering.

"That's a very good question, Bradbury. Nelson is a troublemaker! Whereas the rest of you are taking your first day like men, he has started off by behaving like a spoilt brat," he said. Basher nodded his head in agreement.

"But where is he?" Geordie White asked. Bulldog glared at him, so Geordie added, "Please Sergeant."

"That's better," Bulldog said, then, "He'll spend the night in 'the Cooler' and he can thank his lucky stars that I'm a forgiving sort of chap, or he would be put away for a long time for assault."

After hearing this, we thought that maybe Bulldog wasn't so bad after all. He would prove to be extremely hard, but fair, unless crossed. Derek had obviously rubbed the Sergeant up the wrong way.

We recruits spent that afternoon cleaning our rifles. Each man had his own rifle, housed in a 'rack', down the centre aisle of the billet. Basher showed us how to disassemble the rifles, oil them, then re-assemble them. He also reminded us of our responsibility for looking after our own weapons.

We had dinner at 1700 hours and after that we all thought the rest of the evening would be our own. Unfortunately, we had forgotten about 'fatigues': Thanks to F/L Burke, everyone in the billet had to spend the evening on duty. Geordie White, three others and I had to help in the mess. There were thousands of potatoes to peel, floors to scrub and many other tasks to perform. What a first day! The one good thing to come out of working in the mess was that after finishing all the chores the Chef prepared steak and chips for all of us.

On the second day the early morning ritual was virtually the same. Wake up at 5.30, wash and shave in cold water, clean and polish the billet, then march to breakfast and back again. The main difference being that 'Birk' did not inspect the billet, thank goodness.

"After breakfast Basher came into the billet and shouted, "Stand by your beds, ready for inspection!"

This time Bulldog made the inspection. As you may have gathered by now, a tough guy, a stickler for discipline, but did not wet his finger, nor indeed did he run it along the top of the lockers! Just before we were due to go outside on parade, Derek turned up. He looked a bit bruised about the face, but appeared none the worse for his ordeal. Geordie and I greeted him.

"What happened Derek, did they beat you up?"

"Of course not," Derek replied haughtily, "These bruises were earned when I fought with the SPs."

"Don't brag, Derek," Geordie said. "You don't want to get into more trouble do you?"

Derek shrugged his shoulders and said defiantly,

"They will not break me!"

"I do wish you would be like the rest of us and try to put up with it." I pleaded with him. "The training will only last for eight weeks."

All the rest of the men in the billet tried to reason with Derek, but to no avail, then Basher called,

"Outside on parade!"

Derek would only be with us for another week, but during that time he had caused so much trouble for himself and the others that the airmen were glad to see the back of him. One particular morning when Basher gave the order to go outside on parade, Derek refused to go and had to be escorted to the

CO's office. He ended his service with a court martial and left the service in disgrace. Service life obviously didn't suit him!

Although life was pretty tough at RAF West Kirby, we were starting to become accustomed to it. After three weeks of continuous square-bashing, physical training and obstacle courses, I felt fitter than ever before. Twice a week, on a Wednesday and Saturday, I went dancing with half a dozen of my friends. We had found a little village, just a short bus ride from West Kirby and, apart from a small band I had formed, it turned out to be the only form of relaxation we found during our period of training. There was a quaint little dance hall, holding a maximum of one hundred people, the music provided by an old record-player, the only consolation being that a few of the local girls went there and that made a welcome relief for us!

During the fourth week I received a letter from Auntie, informing me that Ruth would be getting married, not to Alan, much to her surprise, but to a carpenter called Ronnie Moss. I applied for compassionate leave, but the RAF turned down my request because Ruth did not qualify as an immediate relative. I felt extremely disappointed, but wrote back to Auntie, offering my congratulations.

During the same week we had our first period of Rifle Range training. Many of the airmen became quite proficient but I couldn't hit the side of a barn from ten paces! The Sergeant at Arms couldn't understand what I was doing wrong until it dawned on him that I consistently closed the wrong eye when taking aim!

It was Coronation Year, 1953, and if I had joined up two months earlier I would have been part of the 'Parade Proper' in London. As it happened, the Queen paid a visit to Llangollen, Wales and our 'Crack Squad' had been chosen to represent the Squadron. This would involve a lot of hard work on 'The Square', for all of us. We would be lining the route into and out of the town, forming a 'Guard of Honour'. Even so, my friends and I were really proud to have this privilege. Although we had very few evenings free, now that the big event drew close, we still had some time for relaxation.

I had struck lucky in one respect. Three other musicians were stationed at West Kirby with me. Fred and Stan were going to train as Medical Orderlies but Fred played jazz piano and Stan beat the drums. So the not-so-famous 'Hatters' evolved. At the same time there appeared at the camp a reasonable trumpeter called Hans who hailed from Austria, but had lived with his parents in England for a number of years. The Hatters were a Dixieland Band who, for the last few weeks of Basic Training, became extremely popular with everyone at West Kirby. It had been decided to use the NAAFI for the venue for the dances. Many of the local girls were invited on Saturday nights to attend dances there, and on Wednesday the WRAF substituted. At last I seemed to be making some headway towards achieving my musical ambitions. For the moment, though, I had to concentrate on the job at hand…

After three weeks of preparation and hard work, the 'Big Day' arrived. The Order of the Day – up at 0400 hours, wash, shave and dress, then go to the cookhouse for breakfast. The cooks seemed to have made a special effort. The milk on the cornflakes actually tasted like the real thing, for once! The egg and bacon did not seem quite so greasy as normal, even the tea had cow's milk in it instead of from a tin. Having finished our breakfast we returned to the billet to put the finishing touches to our 'Ceremonial Uniforms'. Even though the 'Air Force Best Blue' did not seem as resplendent as the Guards' uniforms, after all the 'bulling', the airmen were quite eye-catching. The No.1 uniforms were put into dust-covers, the boots shining brightly, into holdalls along with the 'Blancoed' white webbing belts and gaiters. Each man had a packed lunch prepared by the cooks, for it certainly would be a long day. The normal mode of transport was by ten-tonner, but on that day there had been a service coach laid on for each 'Flight'.

After a two-hour journey I arrived, along with five-hundred other airmen, at Llangollen. There were thousands of people, many of whom had been waiting for hours to see Her Majesty the Queen. Unfortunately for them and the occasion it started to drizzle, and the forecast for the day did not augur well. Many in the bustling crowd were wearing traditional Welsh Costumes in beautiful colours.

The coaches pulled into a car park, near to the starting point of the procession, to allow the men to change into their 'ceremonials'. There would be frustratingly long wait before the Royal Party arrived. We had all arrived early and the clock only showed 0900, the Queen not being due until 1400 hours.

The Guard of Honour marched to the starting point, then the men were placed facing each other in two's, twelve feet apart, on opposite sides of the road, all along the route that Her Majesty would be taking. We were ordered to 'Stand at Ease' by Basher, and finally, 'Stand Easy'. This meant we could relax, but must not move our feet. Each man had his rifle in his right hand, with its 'butt' resting on the ground. We were going to have to stand on the same spot, for seven hours, an extreme test of endurance! Bulldog instructed us to find something green, to fix our eyes upon, for example, a tree. Having to stand for such a long time without being able to move, meant that somebody would be likely to faint. Looking at a green object helps to relax the eyes, also the nerves of the body. If either Basher or Bulldog discovered that anyone had not eaten breakfast they would have put them on a 'charge', as it is an offence in the Armed Forces to miss breakfast parade. It does make sense though, on reflection, especially when servicemen and women, had to undergo such endurance tests. From time to time, just to relieve the monotony, Bulldog put 'The Guard of Honour' through its paces, by performing some Arms Drill.

"Squa...d, properly at ease. Pay attention now, Squa...d, atten...tion! Squa...d, shoulde...r arms! Por...t arms! Should...r arms, slope arms! Stand a...t ease! Stand easy."

At 1300 hours, Basher and Bulldog walked along the ranks and handed out mugs of hot tea, which at least helped to keep out the cold. Unfortunately, one or two of the men had fainted, which really was to be expected. If this had happened during the Royal Procession they would have been put on a charge, but luckily it happened prior to that.

At 1400 hours, the Royal Party appeared, accompanied by the cheers of the thousands of onlookers. The Guard of Honour snapped to attention as Her Majesty drove slowly by in an open-top car, enabling her to see and be seen by Her Subjects. The opportunity to see Her Majesty at such close quarters gave me quite a thrill. I had to look to the front, as did the rest of the Guard of Honour, but I still managed to see her clearly – just a fleeting glimpse though.

After the royal car had passed by, another two hours elapsed before we airmen were dismissed. Apart from the drizzle earlier, the weather had remained kind to us, so the visit went by unspoiled. It had been a long, exhausting day, so after a hot meal in the local Territorial Army Barracks, the rest of the Squadron, including me, were on our way back to West Kirby.

The only big occasion remaining before the eight weeks' training had been completed was the 'Passing Out Parade'. I could hardly believe that the end had nearly arrived! In a way I would be sorry to leave, not that I had made many friends, but the discipline and training had made me feel like a new person. The Passing Out Parade went according to everyone's expectations.

I had now become a fully-fledged airman, ready and eager to start my musical career in the Royal Air Force.

After the big parade, we airmen returned to our billets and were able, finally, to relax completely. I lay on my bed, dreaming of playing with the RAF Central Band, when both Bulldog and Basher burst into the billet.

"Off your beds, you miserable shower!" they both shouted at once, so everyone leapt off their beds.

'What's going on?' I thought, 'The Passing Out Parade went well and even the Camp CO had complimented us on our turn-out and marching.'

"Outside on parade!" Bulldog bellowed.

"Double quick!" Basher yelled, so we all adjusted our uniforms, and rushed outside.

"Flight... attention!" Bulldog shouted. "Into line righ...t turn. By the right, quick march, left, right, left, right, left, right, left..."

I felt so tired I could hardly move my legs, but I knew the penalty for faltering.

"Break into double time!" Bulldog bawled.

I couldn't really understand what was happening, but would soon be finding out.

We twenty-six men were rushed past 'The Square' and then, eventually, Bulldog shouted, "Squa...d, halt!"

I couldn't believe my eyes. We had stopped outside the Sergeants' Mess.

'I wonder what we are doing here?' I thought.

"Into line, righ...t turn," Bulldog ordered, then shouted "Hats off!" then continued, "Quick march, left, right, left, right, left, right, left..."

As we stepped into the Sergeants' Mess, Bulldog said, "Well done lads, you're the best bunch I've ever had the pleasure of training!"

We enjoyed the best meal we had eaten for eight weeks, followed by plenty of free beer. What a wonderful way to say goodbye to West Kirby!

4. First Steps

During my week's leave, I spent most of the time practising. I also wrote to Auntie to apologise for not being able to come to see them, just yet. Dad had just bought me a new clarinet. My old 'Regent' had been good enough for a beginner, but not for a player of my standard! Dad had been lucky, being able to purchase two clarinets, one for me and one for himself, at a moderate cost. The instruments were Boosey and Hawkes 1010's. Boosey, at that time, were the largest makers of musical instruments in the world.

I had received notice to appear for an audition in front of the Officer in Charge of the Royal Air Force School of Music, based at Uxbridge, a Flight Lieutenant Wallace. I felt terribly excited. At long last I would be achieving my lifelong ambition to be a musician and play with a professional band.

The RAF School of Music was only a short rail journey away from my home at Neasden. On the day of the audition, I boarded the 'tube' at Neasden Station, changing at Wembley Park onto the Metropolitan Line, bound for Uxbridge. I arrived at my destination half an hour before my audition was to take place and reported to the SP sergeant at the Guardroom.

"Do you know the way to the Music Services HQ?" the Sergeant asked me.

"No Sergeant, I haven't been here before," I replied.

"Come along with me and I'll show you," the NCO said.

I thanked him, so we walked the one and a half miles, to the Band HQ. The Sergeant handed me over to the clerk at the Band Orderly Room, then bade me farewell. Corporal

Paddy Maloney, a cheery-faced Irishman, had known my Dad well and reminisced of the times when they had been stationed at Uxbridge together. After a long wait he ushered me into F/Lt Wallace's office. The officer asked me some questions before the audition began. He wanted to know why I wished to join the Music Services and apparently seemed satisfied with my reply. After the questions came the Audition.

"Take your clarinet out of the case, Bradbury, then warm up before we commence."

"Yes Sir," I answered respectfully, then took my instrument carefully out of its case and assembled it.

F/Lt Wallace watched me; he seemed impressed by the way that I handled the clarinet.

"It is obvious to me Bradbury, that you love that clarinet," the officer said.

"Yes Sir, I do," I answered.

The audition lasted for one hour and he tested me in every aspect of playing the clarinet.

"First of all, I would like to hear some scales and arpeggios," the officer instructed, then continued, "play for me the scale of C Major." The examiner looked for precision of playing, good rhythm and a basic knowledge of music. Above all, he wanted to hear a round resonant tone. After the scales and arpeggios came some sight-reading: two pieces of music. The first was an exercise to test technique, the second a well known clarinet concerto, by Weber. Finally, I was tested with some theoretical questions.

"What is the meaning of the Italian term *piano*?" he asked.

"To be played quietly, Sir," I replied.

"That is correct," the officer said, smiling.

"What is the Italian equivalent of the English term *Very Loud*?"

"*Fortissimo* Sir," I replied.

"Excellent," the Flight Lieutenant said.

At last the ordeal came to an end. It had been quite a nerve-racking experience for me, but I knew I had done well.

F/Lt Wallace looked directly at me and said, "Well done, Bradbury. I would be most happy, to have you at the Royal Air Force School of Music. Report to Flight Sergeant McCarthy in the Orderly Room at 0800 hours on Monday 1st September."

"Yes Sir!" I replied, bursting with excitement, and rushed home to tell Mum and Dad the good news.

The RAF School of Music Training Course would last twelve months. After that, each qualified musician would be transferred to a Regional Band for the remainder of his service. There were numerous military bands scattered all over England and abroad. Each one had an identification number, for example the band at RAF Locking, Weston-Super-Mare, was the No.1 Regional Band. The Middle East Air Force Band (MEAF), stationed at RAF El Hamra, Canal Zone, Egypt, had been given No.6. First and foremost was, and still is, the RAF Central Band, based at RAF Uxbridge.

There also existed at the time a Women's Royal Air Force Band. They also were stationed at Uxbridge, but as a separate unit. All the bands came under the jurisdiction of Wing Commander A.E. Simms, Organising Director of Music, RAF. His Second in Command, Adjutant Squadron Leader Ward (later to be replaced by Squadron Leader Wallace) was responsible for general discipline.

I reported to the Band Orderly Room at 0800 as directed, and F/S McCarthy took me to the Band Block. I would be living there for the next twelve months. After that, Mac took me to the Clothing Stores to obtain my bedding, then left me to settle in. The Band Block was three-storey building, with rooms that housed three men in each. Each floor had a long corridor, being highly polished. I felt a little disappointed at seeing that. 'Oh no, not more Bull!' I thought, 'I thought I had left all that behind at West Kirby'. Not a bit of it! There would be even more of it in the Music Services. In addition to the School of Music and the Central Band, the Band Block housed one other unit, the RADU, a ceremonial unit used for Royal Functions and State Visits. They formed the Guard of Honour for those special occasions and were just as smart, if not smarter, than any of the top Guards units. The Royal Air Force Drill Unit had the ground floor to themselves, but mixed quite well with the musicians. The Central Bandsmen (though most of them lived out in Married Quarters), occupied the first floor, and the second and third floors were taken up by the School of Music.

After unpacking and making my bed (the same way as at West Kirby) I had lunch and really enjoyed it – none of the sloppy mess that had been served up at Training Camp. After my meal I walked the one and a half miles back to the Band Orderly Room, where I found Corporal Maloney and Mac busy with their paperwork.

"Ah, Bradbury!" Mac greeted me, "Enjoy your lunch?"

"Yes thanks, Flight," I answered, "That certainly is a considerable improvement on the West Kirby mush!"

Paddy and Mac both laughed. The two friends had been in the RAF for many years. They had joined up at the same time and had tasted many service meals in their day.

Paddy was an easy going man, but then he didn't have the same responsibility as Mac. Being in charge of the School of Music (under F/L Wallace of course) with fifty students to look after and discipline taxed his patience to the extreme. F/S McCarthy had to be strict to maintain that discipline.

"This afternoon you will be introduced to Wing Commander Simms, then hear Central Band play." Mac informed me.

"That's just what I have been waiting for," I answered.

"Come along then Bradbury," Mac said, and the two of us went through the Orderly Room, up to a door marked 'Wing Commander A.E. Simms LRAM, ARCM, BM, RAF, Organising Director of Music, Central Band'.

Mac knocked at the big oak-panelled door.

"Come in," the Commanding Officer bellowed.

The Flight Sergeant opened the door and ordered, "Quick march: Left, right, left, right, left...halt!"

Mac turned to Wing Commander Simms, and said, "4128164 Bandsman Bradbury reporting, Sir!"

"At ease Bradbury, stand easy," the CO said to me, then continued, "I want to welcome you to the Royal Air Force Music Services, my lad. I hope you will enjoy your stay with us and that you will pass out of the school with flying colours after your training has been completed."

"Thank you very much Sir," I answered him.

"Dismiss Flight," the CO ordered.

"Very good Sir!" Mac obeyed, then to me, "Properly at ease, att...en...tion. About turn, qu...ck march, left, right, left, right, left."

We visited the main rehearsal next, where the Central Band was already at work. Drum Major Woods conducted the rehearsal until the MD arrived. Mac introduced me to the band, then showed me to a chair, where I could sit and appreciate arguably the best Military Band in the world. First they played the William Tell overture by Rossini, an extremely popular work, both with the public and the musicians themselves. Wing Commander Simms took over the baton for the next number and as he approached the Rostrum the musicians stood to attention.

"Good afternoon, Gentlemen," the MD addressed them, then, "Be seated." He continued... "I want to rehearse the Albert Hall programme for Saturday evening. HRH the Duke of Edinburgh will be there and he has particularly requested Handel's Firework Music. As you all know, on occasions, one of our band comedians, who shall be nameless, gives the audience extra value for their money by playing an extra note in the third bar of the first selection." He looked directly at the first French Horn Player and the whole band rocked with laughter. The Director carried on with his speech... "For the benefit of our guest (looking my way) I would be obliged if you would refrain from tootling on your instruments whilst I am speaking, it is bad manners, as well as showing a lack of professionalism."

That showed the sarcastic side of 'Simmsy', but it had the desired effect. It made me feel quite important, being mentioned by the MD, but the Wing Commander had simply tried to make a point, using me to press it home.

After hearing the remainder of the programme, dinnertime had arrived.

"You' will find your own way back to the Band Block, won't you?" Mac asked.

"Yes Flight Sergeant," I replied. I had enjoyed myself that afternoon and thanked Mac.

"Well, if you want to play as well as that," Mac told me, "You are going to have to work really hard studying, in addition to playing your clarinet."

"I will," I promised.

I returned to the Band Block and met my two roommates, Rick and Barry, who were both clarinettists. Rick came from Nottingham and Barry from Heckmondwyke in Yorkshire. Barry turned out to be my best friend, but Rick proved much harder to get along with. That evening had to be spent 'Bulling' the floors of the rooms and the corridors. Mac inspected the School of Music floors every day. Once a week the whole Block had to be inspected by Wing Commander Simms, then once monthly by the Camp CO, whom also inspected the entire camp. That and Kit

Inspections, were the only things that reminded me of RAF West Kirby, however, the general discipline appeared to be less severe.

By that time, I felt exhausted, so I decided to go to bed early, ready for work the next day. I sat up in bed suddenly! I could hear the sound of a trumpet being played in the Block. Did I say *playing?*' What a terrible noise! At first I thought it must have been an Air Raid Warning. It just came to me that someone had played 'Reveille'. I looked at my watch and saw that it showed 0600 hours. 'Hmm…' I thought, 'That makes a pleasant change. It most certainly is better than being awakened at five-thirty'. The door of the room opened and a head appeared.

"Time to get up lads," the corporal said, chirpily. Bob Pullen, one of the NCOs stationed at Uxbridge taking a course. Bob played the trombone, and along with two other corporals, would be helping Mac to train the students in ceremonial drill, also with the general discipline.

The 'ablutions' were exceptionally modern compared with West Kirby. Although the men had to 'spit and polish' the washrooms themselves, they did not object, as hygiene is most important thing. The first day had passed by so quickly, and before I had time to turn around, it had disappeared.

The trainee musicians climbed out of their beds, washed, dressed, then went to the mess for breakfast. We all had to queue up for our meal, but on arrival at the service-hatch, we found that the plates were pre-heated, waiting for our use! Admittedly, we airmen had to use our own utensils, but I for one preferred that, anyway. 'What an improvement', I thought, 'This is real luxury!' We had a choice of cereals: cornflakes or porridge. The food, served up by cooks in white aprons, appeared to be well cooked. The bacon and egg, did not stick to the plate. In fact, the only thing wrong with the meal was my old enemy, 'margarine', which reared its ugly head once more.

After breakfast, back to the Block to tidy and make the beds up (military fashion), using the 'bumper' on the floors, then 'outside on parade' at 0800. F/S McCarthy inspected the parade, then instructed Cpl Bob, to march us down to the No. 2 Band-room for our first rehearsal. Mac turned up fifteen minutes later and Bob called the Band to attention as the conductor climbed onto the rostrum. The fact that an NCO and not an officer would be conducting the Band made no difference to protocol. Even in civilian life, when a conductor appears before an orchestra it is the done thing for the musicians to stand, as a mark of respect.

"Be seated, men," Mac instructed, then continued, "I wish formally to welcome you to the RAF School of Music. It is going to be extremely tough going, but, after two months of 'Square Bashing', it should not bother you too much. If you keep your heads down, work hard and above all, do as you are told, we are going to get on well together. You are, first and foremost, musicians, but do not forget that you are airmen also. That's the end of my speech; let's get on with the job at hand."

The first piece of music to be played (as one would have expected) was 'Per Ardua ad Astra', the Royal Air Force March. Mac raised his baton and each man raised his instrument instantly. Uniformity of movement, both in marching and of instruments, is absolutely essential for Ceremonial Bands. Obviously, as the musicians were not used to this exercise, the whole thing became a bit of a shambles at first.

I started to feel a little bit impatient, 'Are we never going to start playing?' I thought. At last Mac became satisfied with the unison of movement, raised his baton, then after the 'drum rolls', the band started to play. F/L Wallace had arranged a beautiful 'Trumpet Fanfare' as an introduction to the march. Unfortunately, the Cornet section could not quite handle it, so after a few bars, Mac dropped his hands.

"Cornets, I know that this is the first time that you have seen this music, also that you are just starting your musical career, but that noise startled me, and the rest of the Band, no doubt, the tuning being the worst part of it, and that, as you well know, is the most important part of playing music. Let's try again!"

After a few false starts, the Band played the march from beginning to end. The Flight Sergeant put down his baton and said, "Now that you have warmed up your instruments, I will tune the band."

Mac pulled out a tuning fork from his jacket pocket, then struck the prongs on the back of his hand. Next, he put the tip of the handle onto the music stand that stood in front of him. The vibration produced a resounding note, pitched 'Concert A', for the Oboe. Once the Oboe had been tuned to the note, the rest of the band tuned up to it. Thus, the whole band sounded perfectly in tune. As Mac had stated previously: tuning is the most essential part of musicianship! We continued rehearsing until 10.30, when a NAAFI van drew up outside the band room. That gave us an opportunity, to have a most welcomed cup of tea. It also gave the music students a chance to talk to the Central Band members, whom had been rehearsing in the no. 1 band-room.

The Central Band was going on a tour of the United States of America for three months. This caused a problem, as we students were supposed to be taught by the members of the band. Luckily for us the band had been divided into two sections, 'A' and 'B', hence there were enough musicians of the 'B' band to teach us.

We spent the second half of the morning rehearsing, but after lunch we had to go for a lecture. We went to see a film about the formation of the Royal Air Force (or the Royal Flying Corps, as it had originally been known). Following that, the Education Officer interviewed each of us in turn, to discuss our promotional prospects in the RAF. Of course, this could not possibly happen until each man had passed out of the Music School. He would also have to pass a General Certificate of Education Examination (unless he had already achieved a qualification) before being allowed to sit before the Promotion Board. Unfortunately for me, I had been in such a hurry to leave school that I had not taken any exams other than musical ones.

The daily routine at the RAF School of Music proceeded as in most other jobs except that it could not be described as dull. As previously stated, the Block had to be inspected each day, but after the once-a-week 'Bull Night', keeping the place 'Up to Standard', did not take a great deal of hard work. The Music Students had to line up every morning at 0800 for personal inspection, but apart from that, the general routine did differ from day to day.

The first week at 'The School' passed by fairly quickly. On Friday morning I had my first clarinet lesson from Senior Technician Chesney. 'Ches' was a likeable soul, a man in his early forties, looking forward to retirement from the RAF at the ripe old age of forty-five! As far as I was concerned, the only fault to be found with Ches was that he talked too much, but he was extremely friendly. He was also an excellent teacher and helped me, especially with the theory of music. I mentioned that Ches had the rank of Senior Technician, so for the uninitiated, he wore three stripes upside down on the sleeve of his jacket (unlike the sergeant with stripes the correct way up). The same thing applied to Corporal Technicians, using two chevrons.

The arrangement for lessons with Ches was to have one per week, but not always on the same day. It would depend mainly on the 'B' Band's schedule, as they were very heavily committed, due to the 'A' Band's duties overseas.

The weekend soon arrived and after morning rehearsal the musicians were free until the following Monday. After we had completed one month's training, we were entitled to a weekend pass each, but as we had only completed one week, we would just have to be satisfied with an evening pass. I (along with most of the other young musicians) spent the remainder of Saturday, practising in the ablutions on my clarinet, the only problem being that the acoustics were not really adequate, especially for woodwind players. The washrooms produced an echo, thus giving a false tone to our instruments. We found it difficult, also, to do individual practise, with so many different types of instruments needing to practise at the same time. It became especially awkward, having to compete with 'the Brass'. Poor me, I usually ended up practising in the toilet or in my own room.

On that first Saturday evening, Barry, myself, and a few others went to the dance above 'Burtons the Tailors'. It made a cheap evening out. It needed to be, as we students were only paid seven shillings and sixpence per week. After the evening meal in the Mess, my friends and I changed into 'civvies' and went to the Eight Bells for a drink, before heading for the dancehall. Being situated on the other side of the road and directly opposite the camp, the pub was a popular venue, so as my friends and I walked in, we found the bar packed out. We ordered our drinks and sat down at a corner table underneath a window.

"This is a smashing little boozer!" Brian exclaimed.

"Tha's reet, tha' knows, Barry agreed in his strong Yorkshire dialect.

I laughed at him. He had a similar accent to that of Uncle Walt, except that Uncle had a Lancashire one, much stronger and very much harder to understand.

Bob spoke up next. "Did you know that some of the Central Band boys are playing at the dance?" he asked.

"Are they really? I enquired.

"Yes," Bob replied, "And you'll never guess, who else is playing."

"No – who?" we all chimed in together.

"Ronnie Scott is one of the guest artistes," Bob continued, "And apparently, Tommy Whittle, is the other tenor sax… and to top it all, Don Lang will be there, on trombone."

"Let's go gang," I said, so we finished our drinks and moved on to the dance. After paying the entrance fee of 2/6d each, the friends ambled into the small hall. It only accommodated one hundred people at the most. We were most surprised to see that the band, a sextet, was entirely comprised of Central Band musicians. The boys of the band acknowledged us and, after exchanging a few pleasantries, my friends and I settled onto the benches around the perimeter of the hall.

Musically speaking, the band sounded excellent, nothing out of the ordinary, but pleasant to listen to. At 0730 Ronnie Scott and Tommy Whittle played some progressive jazz, along with Don Lang on trombone. They were accompanied by piano, string bass and drums, and they really did bring the place to life. Their first number 'Battle of the Saxes', was fiery to say the least. No use in trying to dance to the music, for one thing we wouldn't have been able to keep up with the speed, and for another, the hall had filled to capacity. The next was another popular number, 'Lullaby of Birdland', and the three guest musicians really 'went to town' on that one. My pals and I listened enviously, although 'Big Band Jazz' is more to my taste. Even so, I did find it all rather exciting!

The weekend soon passed and Monday arrived again. After Mac had made his daily inspection of the School Quarters and the personal inspection had been concluded, he shocked everyone by saying, "Right lads, get changed for Physical Training."

"Oh, Flight!" we lads all moaned at the same time, "It's too cold for PT."

"Tough!" Mac answered, "Anyone not changed and outside in ten minutes, will be on a charge."

"Parade…" Cpl Bob shouted, "Par-ade, dismiss!"

In the midst of a mad scramble to get up the stairs to change, in my haste to obey Mac's order, I slipped and fell flat on my face, splitting my lip in the process. Blood poured from my mouth, but as one might have guessed, the thing that worried me the most was the thought of not being able to play. Both Mac and Bob helped me to my feet.

"Trust you, Bradbury!" Mac said, unsympathetically, "Get him to the sick bay, Corporal, double quick."

"Right away, Flight," Bob answered, then rushed me the quarter mile to see the camp MO.

"That's a hard way to get out of PT," Bob said, grinning.

"Is n' joke," I tried to say, but couldn't properly. I had to have stitches in my lip, stopping me from playing, for at least two weeks.

I spent three days in the camp hospital, situated at the far end of the camp, close to the 'Married Quarters'. After being discharged from hospital, I had no alternative but to play the cymbals at rehearsals and parades until my lip completely healed. That did not please me one little bit, but I soon made up for it when my lip got better.

The weeks turned into months and already six months had passed, since I had first arrived at RAF Uxbridge. I had been home on a couple of weekend passes, but I soon began to miss my Auntie. I wondered what Ruth's husband looked like. I would have to make sure that I visited my relations on my next leave. I wrote to them every week and Auntie repeatedly asked, 'When are you coming to see us?'

During the twelve months I spent at the School of Music, one moment stands out in my mind. I had overslept, due to playing at a dance the evening before, and I did something that I had never done before, I forgot to shave! One would think that one of my friends might have pointed it out to me, but nobody did. F/S McCarthy called the students to go on parade, then proceeded to inspect us. When he came to me, he looked closely at me and said, "Student Bradbury, is there a new law in the RAF, instructing Airmen to grow beards?" I froze, then felt my face, 'Oh my goodness!' I thought, 'I haven't shaved'.

"Why Bradbury, have you not shaved?" Mac shouted furiously.

"I overslept and in the rush to get dressed, I must have forgotten," I answered nervously.

"Forgotten!" Mac was screaming now. "Forgotten?" He repeated, then continued a little more calmly, "Then all the passes for this weekend will be cancelled and you can blame Bradbury for it."

Cpl Bob spoke up for us.

"I don't think that's very fair, Flight," he said.

"When I want your advice, I will ask for it, Corporal," Mac snapped, still raging.

I couldn't understand, why the others should be punished for something I had done, so I apologised to them, but nobody would speak to me for the remainder of that week.

At the weekend I would be in for a terrible shock. It was Saturday night and I had gone to bed early, partly because I felt so miserable at not being spoken to. I fell asleep, but did not have a restful night. Suddenly, I felt something pressing down on my chest and a feeling of suffocation. The next sensation of being carried, but I couldn't see anything, as something had covered my head. 'Splash – I had been immersed in a bath full of freezing cold water. Everyone gathered around laughing at me. I can see their faces to this day: Mocking, jeering. My best friend Barry wasn't there, but all the others were: Rick, Cpl Bob Pullen, Brian and all the rest of my so-called friends.

I had asked Mac, if I could do fatigues, or something to avoid the others being punished, but he had refused. The Flight Sergeant had known perfectly well what he was doing, when he punished everyone. He knew that the students would in their own way, make me pay the penalty for oversleeping. My good friend Barry pretended to know nothing of the plans to throw me into a bath full of cold water, but I found out later that Barry had been the instigator of the whole thing. I didn't find that out, or other things about my best pal, until a couple of years later. That turn of events made me all the more determined to do well at the School of Music, hoping that the remaining six months would quickly fly by. One thing was for certain – I wouldn't ever forget to shave again!

The RAF held the camp parade once per week, and the School had to alternate with Central Band in providing the music, for the March Past and Inspection. To prepare for this, the students had to have Ceremonial Drill, playing both on the march and static. We were of course trained in special movements, whilst playing on the march. The drill consisted of Counter-Marching, the Band split into five marching columns, then on the command, 'Band ...Counter-March', the trombonists, who were at the head of each column, would raise their instruments to signal that they were about to turn. Each column leader then had to turn left, making an arc and marching to the rear. The men behind, had to follow suit until the ranks were turned inside out (so as to speak). This can be seen at any Military Tattoo or Marching Display. 'It's difficult enough playing whilst on the march', I thought, 'But imagine what it would be like playing on horseback!'

That year, 1953, saw a very bad winter, and there were more parades than usual. By December each parade on the square, became tougher than the one before. One day, the Band were marching the 'Camp' onto parade, when it started to snow. I had a metal clarinet, which had been issued especially for outdoor playing. It just so happened on that occasion, the saliva froze as it ran out of the Clarinet bell, forming into icicles. Most of the instruments seized up, but the musicians were not allowed to leave the Square, until the Parade had come to an end.

At Christmas, the students were given one week's leave, so I went home to Neasden. Dad had time off from the Dance Orchestra, so for once the whole family would be together, for the 'Festive Season' I would not be having much time off for enjoyment, as I had plenty of studying to do, in preparation for my final exams at the end of May.

"I wonder where I'll be posted to?" I asked my Dad.

"Hopefully, you'll stay at Uxbridge, in the Central Band," Dad answered, then went on, "Let's hope they don't send you to RAF Catterick, where the Regiment is stationed."

I also hoped that wouldn't happen.

"There's been talk about some of us being sent overseas," I said.

"Don't you have to volunteer for that, Peter?" my Mum asked.

"I'm not quite sure Mum, but I expect I'll soon find out when my training is over," I answered.

I enjoyed my Christmas at home, but felt glad to get back to camp. The sooner I returned, the sooner my year would be up, then I would be playing music all the time, or so I thought.

The big day arrived and I had passed my Practical and Theoretical exams with flying colours, so I applied for a permanent posting with RAF Central Band. Unfortunately, they were over-strength, so unless I applied for an overseas posting I would have no option other than to go to Catterick. Some of the boys had applied for a Far Eastern posting to RAF Changi, Singapore. Others for the No. 6 Regional Band at Eel Hamra, Egypt. Barry had applied for the latter, so as we were supposed to be friends, I did likewise. We were both accepted. Myself, Barry, Rick (unfortunately), Brian and a few others were to go to the Middle East. That decision would soon cause trouble with my mum, but I had to sort my own life out.

Three weeks before we were due to fly abroad, we Musicians 2nd class (as we were then known), had to have our injections. The Far East contingent had Malaria jabs and I, along with the Middle East Volunteers, had the Yellow Fever ones. In the room opposite to me lived a tenor sax player called Johnny. He had been given the Malaria jab and it resulted in poor Johnny having nightmares. In the middle of the night his friend and room-mate woke up to hear Johnny screaming. When Brian opened his eyes, he saw his friend standing on the window ledge (three floors up), stark naked and ready to jump. Brian grabbed Johnny, thereby saving his life.

We musicians were given a fortnight's leave in which to prepare for our departure abroad. I would, at last, be going to see Auntie, Uncle Walt and Ruth again. My Auntie could hardly contain her excitement when I wrote to tell her that I would soon be coming. I went home first and spent a couple of days, with my family. My sister had grown fast (four years of age now, and had long blonde wavy hair). Christine attended Ballet School and Mum had enrolled her at Ada Foster's Acting and Drama School, Blackbird's Cross, Neasden. My sister looked really pleased to see me and I lovingly fussed over her. Mum became upset when I announced that I would be going to Egypt. The Canal Zone had become a trouble spot and I would soon be heading towards it. There were problems in Cyprus between the Greeks and the Turks, trouble in Kenya with the Mau Mau, and skirmishes virtually everywhere in the Middle East, but that didn't worry me overmuch. I felt quite secure in the knowledge that being a musician I surely wouldn't have to fight... well I hoped not, anyway!

"You'll have to be a stretcher bearer if there's any fighting," Dad said.

"Gee thanks, Dad," I retorted, "You certainly know how to cheer a fellow up!"

"Well, it's true, that's what happened during the war, anyhow," Dad went on.

"We will have to wait and see," I replied.

Grace looked upset.

"Why did you have to volunteer for the Middle East, with all that fighting going on and everything?" she asked tearfully.

"I'm sorry Mum, if I had known that it would upset you so much, I would have put in for Catterick, although I just did not fancy going there, especially after all I've heard about the place. Mind you, Flying Officer Hutchinson, Ex-Bandmaster of Catterick, is going with us to Egypt, and I hear that he's quite a tough customer.

I sat in the railway carriage by myself, as usual, looking out of the window and listening to the wheels going clickety-clack, clickety-clack ... going abroad ... will I come back ... clickety-clack ... then I dozed off.

I really did look forward to seeing the Jackson family again. Uncle met me, at Piccadilly Station, Manchester, just as he had done all those years before.

"Ee by gum lad, t'is grand t' se' thee," my Uncle said, hugging me.

"It is great to see you again, Uncle and I am sorry that it has been so long," I replied.

"By 'eck, t'is champion t' se' thee, in tha' uniform!" Walt continued, "Y'r Auntie c'n 'ardly wait, t' se' thee."

"Let's hurry then, Uncle," I said excitedly.

Auntie stood waiting patiently by the gate.

"Hello Doll-y-o luv," she cried, as she grabbed and kissed me.

"You can't call me that now, Auntie," I said feeling a little embarrassed, after all, I am nearly nineteen now, not three and a half years old anymore!"

"You will always be little Doll-y-o to me," Auntie replied, with tears in her eyes, "You looked just like a little doll, standing there, with a label around your neck and I'll never think of you, as anything else, as long as I live."

I knew that this would always be my real home and wished that I had not been forced to leave, but all that was history now.

The Jacksons had a new address now. With Ruth getting married and Auntie's legs giving her a heap of trouble, Uncle had decided that they should move to a smaller house without any hills to climb. The house was situated at No.6 Greenbank Terrace, Stacksteads, just about a five minute ride from Bacup, so Auntie would still be able to see her friends and relations. Along with Walt and Ruth, they kept her going.

The house had a black lead stove, which brought back fond memories to me. It consisted of three bedrooms, a living room cum dining room, a scullery with a small gas cooker, plus one upstairs bedroom. It had a cellar, of course, most houses in those days had one (complete with coal-chute). The only problem was that the toilet had been built at the bottom of the garden.

All in all it was a cosy little place, the reason being due to the fact that Auntie lived in it. She could have made even a dungeon seem snug. Due to the lack of space in the house, I had to sleep on the sofa, but I didn't care as I felt so comfortable at being there again. Auntie made us a nice cup of tea, then we relaxed and chatted over old times.

"Do you ever see anything of Sean?" I asked.

"The family moved back to Ireland," Auntie answered.

"Did I tell you that I saw Lottie, when I went to Clacton on holiday?" I asked my Auntie.

"No you didn't tell us, Dear," Auntie replied. "How is the sweet little thing?"

"Not so little, Auntie, she is quite a young woman now," I concluded.

After a good night's sleep, I felt refreshed, even though I had awakened at 0400, having a mug of hot tea thrust into my hand. Uncle thought that I might like one, for old time's sake. Walt still had the same job, at the Felt Works at Waterfoot. 'Gosh he does work hard', I thought. I didn't feel like getting up at that early hour of the morning, but as poor Uncle Walt struggled to move around I felt guilty, and did rouse myself. I folded the blankets and sheets up (not in military fashion, I might add) then proceeded to get dressed.

We spent the first day, getting some shopping for Auntie, then generally familiarising myself with the old 'haunts'. I thought I might see someone from the past, who I would know.

"All the boys and girls that you knew have grown up, as you have," Auntie explained, "And they have either got married, returned to London to their parents, or just moved elsewhere. One or two of the older people will remember you, I'm sure, but whether or not you will remember them, I'm not so sure."

"It doesn't really matter," I said, "I have come to see all of you... no one else."

That evening, while we were sitting and drinking tea (as usual) Ruth arrived with her husband, Ronnie Moss. She hadn't changed much since our last meeting, her hair just as fiery red, bright eyes and jolly nature. She was so happy to see me.

"I have some good news for you, dear," she said to me, "I'm going to have a baby."

"I'm so pleased for you," I replied, "And that will make Grandparents of Auntie and Uncle, for the first time."

Ruth looked at her Mother and Father and smiled, "You will make a lovely Nannie and Grandad," she remarked.

The evening had quite a mild feel, at least by comparison with the normally cold, blustery weather 'Up North'. I decided that I would like to go for a walk across the moors, so the three of us, Ruth, Ronnie and I, set off.

I reminisced with Ruth.

"This is just like old times," I said.

"It certainly is," she answered, remembering the long walks that she and I had taken those many years ago.

"Do you remember the Reservoir and the Old Haunted House?" Ruth asked me.

"Do I?" I exclaimed, "I fell into the Reservoir and would have drowned if it hadn't been for Sean," I continued, shivering, "And that house always did give me the creeps."

After walking for thirty minutes, the trio reached the Reservoir. Ronnie spoke first.

"I've never been this way before."

"I have, many times," I said and related my story to Ronnie.

"You were extremely lucky," Ruth's husband replied, "And what of this 'Haunted House?' he questioned me.

"All make believe, really," I answered, "Whether or not a ghost existed, is cause for some speculation," I concluded.

Ruth took up the story...

"Legend has it that the house had been inhabited by a midget who, due to his family tradition, had been forced to marry his cousin. He didn't love her, but being a kind man had accepted his fate gracefully. His wife desperately wanted a child, but was unable to bear children.

One day whilst out horse riding, Hildegarde fell from her mount and twisted her ankle. As she lay writhing in agony, a small voice called out to her, "Are you hurt, don't be frightened, we'll help you?" Hildegarde looked around, but could see nothing. Suddenly, she felt herself being hoisted into the air and carried, at great speed, through the forest. Although quite small, Hildegarde realised that something even smaller than she was transporting her along. As she looked down, she saw that the force carrying her turned out to be an army of ants.

Ronnie interrupted her.

"Come off it Ruth, luv... that's rubbish."

Ruth glared at her husband.

"I did say 'legend has it that the story is true' not that I *believed* it dear," she retorted angrily.

"Sorry, carry on then," Ronnie urged her.

Ruth continued with the story... "As I was saying... Hildegarde was being moved along by an army of ants, then out of the trees stepped her husband, Karl. He had been transformed from the mild mannered man that she knew. His face had become twisted, and resembled an ant more than a man.

"Take her to the house," Karl ordered the ants.

"What are you going to do with me?" Hildegarde begged, nervously. Her husband didn't answer, but hurried towards his home as if there were wild animals chasing after him. As they disappeared into the house, never to be seen again, an old man passing by saw that amazing spectacle. He swore that two days later he observed thousands of ants swarming in and out of every window of the house and within one week the house fell into ruins. It did seem as if Hildegarde had her wish, to bear children, after all!"

Ronnie and I both laughed at that ridiculous story, but the three of us had a long look at the ruins, before going on our way.

5. Life Abroad

On September 6th 1954, one month prior to my 19th birthday, I reported to Central Band HQ at Uxbridge, ready for the flight to Egypt. The band had assembled at No.1 Bandroom at 0700 hours and the Bandmaster, Flying Officer Hutchinson, his second-in-command Sergeant Whipps and Corporal Pullen were there to organise the proceedings. The Band consisted of 29 musicians: the Bandmaster, Band Sergeant, Corporal, fifteen graduates from the School of Music, plus eleven musicians picked from Regional Bands scattered throughout Great Britain.

The transport arrived at 0800 and the loading up commenced. What a performance – with all the instruments, music, music stands and personal luggage. Finally, the two coaches and a ten-ton lorry were ready to proceed to their destination, RAF Lyneham, Wiltshire, en-route for Egypt. 'No.6 Regional Band MEAF' would be staying in the transit camp at RAF Lyneham overnight and were due to leave at 0600 the following morning.

Feeling terribly excited, I jumped out of bed early, looking forward to the flight, but at the same time feeling a little apprehensive. My thoughts were interrupted by the Sergeant shouting, "Come on lads, outside, let's get the plane loaded!"

The flight had been scheduled to take thirteen hours plus stops, the only breaks were going to be for re-fuelling and to allow the passengers to take in a hot meal. The aeroplane, a RAF 'Valetta' twin-engined freight carrier, had been converted to carry passengers, luggage and equipment.

The band finally took to the air on a cold, wet day, typical of September in England. I felt a trifle nervous, as I had not spent much time in the air to date, but then again neither had any of the other musicians. I certainly wasn't the only one to feel that way, in fact, if the truth had been known, most of the passengers were feeling a little jittery! As always there were the 'Smart Alecs' – you know the sort – nothing worries them, they just laugh and make ridiculous remarks, such as 'It's alright, don't worry if one of the wings drops off, there is another one! There were a few of that type in the Band, but luckily, nobody took any notice of them.

The large, noisy aircraft took to the sky and its passengers, including myself, were off to start a new life abroad...

During the flight there were strict rules. Passengers were only allowed to walk about the aircraft two at one time. The crew consisted of just a pilot and co-pilot, there were no hostesses or stewards on military aircraft. Pre-packed sandwiches and drinks had been prepared for the passengers in the cookhouse at Lyneham. After we had been airborne for two hours I began to feel a little peckish so I unwrapped my sandwiches and, discovering that they were my favourite, cheese, chewed away contentedly, looking out of the porthole at the dark, uninviting water far down below. The plane carrying the MEAF Band, touched down on the runway of RAF Luqa in Malta at 1600 hours local time. The passengers were allowed one hour to have a meal and relax while the plane re-fuelled and the flight engineer checked it over. We had our first experience of the intense heat, the temperature being 90 degrees Fahrenheit in the shade. After enjoying a reasonable meal, the Band set off again.

The next stop was RAF Nicosia in Cyprus. The complete journey, including stops, should only have taken sixteen hours, but with some slight engine trouble, and longer breaks than scheduled, the band would be four hours overdue on arrival in Egypt. After light refreshments, the band started the final stage of its journey and landed at RAF Fayid at 0400 hours local time. RAF Fayid being a Transit Camp, this allowed us to rest overnight before making the short journey by road to RAF El Hamra.

On arrival we were given bedding and shown to a large marquee where all of us just flopped out with exhaustion. We were awakened at 0700 by the Camp Bugler playing 'Reveille'. The first task of the day, after breakfast, was to unload the aeroplane, then to transfer the load onto lorries.

RAF El Hamra, situated only a walking distance from the Suez Canal, was a gigantic place. This would be my home for the next eighteen months.

'What a desolate place', I thought, 'right in the middle of the desert. What have I let myself in for?'

Many different sections of the Royal Air Force were stationed at El Hamra; the Medical Corps, the Signal Corps, and even the RAF Service Police (SPs). Also stationed there were many Army Units, including the famous Black Watch, the KOYLIs and, last but not least, a French Parachute Regiment. One could only imagine what would happen if trouble erupted between that lot! It so happened that there were quite a few skirmishes, especially after they had all been drinking in the NAAFI.

I could hardly believe my eyes when I first set eyes on my home for the next eighteen months – a tent! Twenty tents were laid out in rows of five in a small compound far away from everyone else in the camp. For some peculiar reason the bands were always tucked away in the farthest corner of the camps, perhaps because the noise of their practising upset everyone. One thing was for certain, there would be nobody to disturb in that corner of the wilderness! The SPs had been using the Band Compound previously, but they had now been moved to a different part of the camp.

Each tent housed two musicians, leaving six of them empty. The Bandmaster had been billeted in the Officer's Mess, and Sergeant Whipps in the Sergeants Mess. That left Corporal Bob Pullen with a tent to himself. The tents were pitched across concrete bases, each three feet high, with two steps at the entrance. Two tent poles supported the tarpaulin roof, which had been anchored by tying cords to the metal rings fixed to each base. The tents were reasonably secure, but when the *khamsin*[2] raged we musicians were sometimes left without a roof over our heads, but generally the tents remained intact. Each tent had a small surround made of empty jerrycans. Each can had to be painted white, which did seem silly, as every time a sandstorm blew up they were covered over with sand, so had to be dug out and painted once more.

For the first weeks, the Black Watch remained the only regiment close to our band, the regimental 'reveille' being played on the bagpipes at 0400 hours, so I and my fellow musicians were relieved when they were transferred to a different part of the camp.

For the first three months in Egypt the lads did not tour around. The only occasions we left camp, except to go swimming, were to play for parades or concerts in other parts of the Canal Zone.

Flying Officer Hutchinson only stayed with our band for one month, then Flying Officer Wagner (the W not being pronounced V, unlike the great composer) replaced him. The former had to return to England on compassionate grounds and we musicians eagerly awaited the arrival of our replacement Bandmaster. F/O Wagner turned out to be a strict disciplinarian, but the musicians respected him, mainly due to his musical ability, not because of the way he treated

---

[2] The desert wind.

us. A firm hand turned out to be more necessary in the desert, due to the monotony of life out there. If we were allowed too much freedom we would become lackadaisical and lose our self-esteem (at least that was Waggie's interpretation of discipline).

The first under his command consisted of making up a list of the 'do's and don'ts for the band. He certainly would be making his presence noticed! The band assembled in the Rehearsal Room (a large wooden hut, sectioned off to provide a rehearsal room, band library, plus other rooms). The clock showed 0800 hours and Sgt Whipps read out some of the 'Orders of the Day'.

"Listen in lads," he called out. "Here is the routine for today. First thing, rehearsal until midday, lunch, then individual practice from 1300-1400, followed by siesta (from 0200, when the temperature usually reached 120 degrees Fahrenheit in the shade, providing you could find it! That meant that it would be too hot for anything but sleep.)

We went into the Band Library to collect our music and music-stands, then prepared for our first rehearsal under the command of F/O Wagner.

"Right lads, get set up," Sergeant Whipps ordered.

The band formation was as follows.

Front Row: 2 Solo Bb Clarinets, 2 Repiano Bb Clarinets, 1 second Bb Clarinet, 1 third Bb Clarinet, 1 Concert Flute/Piccolo, 1 Eb Clarinet, 1 Oboe.

Second Row: 2 Solo Bb Cornets, 2 second Bb Cornets, 2 third Bb Cornets, 1 Solo Bb Trombone, 1 second Trombone, 1 third Trombone, 1 Bass Trombone, 1 Euphonium, 1 Alto Sax, 1 Tenor Sax, 2 French Horns, 2 Bb Tubas.

At the Rear: 2 Percussionists (Drums, Tympani, Xylophone etc)

Military Bands usually have thirty-five musicians, sometimes more and occasionally less. The MEAF Band had twenty-eight plus the Bandmaster.

F/O Wagner took up his position on the rostrum and tuned up the band. That operation took some ten minutes, and then we ran through some marches, followed by a couple of light overtures until lunchtime.

The food at El Hamra was, to say the least, terrible and made the food at West Kirby seem good by comparison, although with only two cookhouses to provide for something like two thousand servicemen, it seemed an enormous task. Needless to say, within a few months my weight had dropped from twelve to nine and a half stones.

Due to the hot weather abroad, the musicians had to wear different clothing from that worn in England. The normal working dress was 'Khaki Drill', consisting of shorts or trousers with short-sleeved shirts, long socks and the normal blue beret. For ceremonial occasions or Officers' Mess functions, or indeed any other special occasion, we had to wear a white ceremonial uniform with a blue-peaked cap.

The Remembrance Service at El Alamein was our first official function outside the Canal Zone. Virtually the whole of Middle Eastern Command, Canal Zone turned out there. The rehearsals were exhausting, every morning except Saturday and Sunday being spent either on the Parade Ground with the rest of the Camp or individual sections, executing marching practice. The heat became intolerable, even before 1400 hours, usually about 90 degrees Fahrenheit.

On the day, No. 6 Regional Band MEAF gathered all its equipment together and climbed into a ten-ton lorry in readiness for our journey to El Alamein via Tel-Al-Kabir railway station. The journey would take approximately eight hours. We arrived at the station, loaded the equipment onto the train, and were on our way. The railway carriages were converted cattle trucks and the journey turned out to be the most uncomfortable I had ever experienced. I did, however, manage to snatch one hour of sleep on the way. A sharp jolt awakened me as the train came to a sudden halt, but the sight of the station through the window made me think I must be dreaming! It was the famous station at Zagazig, where everything was made of white marble, even the platform. The faces peering at me through the window made things worse, the women, in their *yashmaks*, with just their eyes and the tiniest amount of olive skin showing, the Arab men in *jalabahs* and turbans, appearing extremely ferocious, although there was nothing to fear. The train soon moved on its way again.

The train pulled into the makeshift station at El Alamein, and there another amazing sight met our gaze. For miles, as far as the eye could see, there were tanks, lorries and guns of every description, strewn across the desert. Although the war had been over for nine years, there were so many land mines and unexploded bombs that it would be too dangerous to attempt to retrieve them for scrap metal. Occasionally, there would be an explosion, as an unlucky desert creature, perhaps a camel, would tread on one and set it off.

I felt really tired after that long journey, but before I could rest or have anything to eat, the tents had to be pitched. The Band, as everyone else, had to use our sleeping bags that night. The toilet facilities were even worse than at El Hamra. There were only buckets with screens around them to afford some privacy. By now my fellow musicians and I had become used to 'roughing it' but one would have thought that nine years after the end of the war, conditions might have improved for servicemen abroad. Attempting to shave proved another difficult task, but had to be accomplished somehow. Each man had been given a large container of fresh water, which had to be utilised for drinking, washing and shaving.

Luckily, we would only have to shave once before returning to base at El Hamra. We had been issued with 'mess-tins' – two anti-rust metal containers with flexible handles, twelve inches long by six inches deep. Using a bench to rest them on and a mirror suspended from the tent-pole, my tent mates and I managed, eventually, to shave ourselves.

The night passed uneventfully (apart from the pyard dogs howling and the occasional explosion as another luckless creature set off a mine) with a still sky and nothing to worry about. I fell asleep, dreaming of white marble buildings with gigantic pillars and faces peering at me.

I awakened next morning and was just about to get out of my sleeping bag when I just froze! My right hand trailed in the sand and there beside it lay a scorpion.

'Oh my goodness,' I thought, 'Is this my time to die?'

Luckily for me it was the scorpion that had died somehow. It must have been lying there the night before, but due to the lack of light in the tent I had failed to see it. With a shiver, I leapt out of my sleeping-bag, washed, dressed and made final preparations for the parade.

The next item on the agenda was to hurry to the big marquee for cereal followed by bread and jam. One thing you could always rely on in the Forces was a cup of hot tea, no matter how difficult the circumstances.

The Remembrance Day Parade to commemorate the 'fallen' at El Alamein commenced at 0730 hours. Field Marshall Montgomery officiated at the ceremony, arriving at 0800. Unfortunately for the Band, with the sun behind us, reflecting onto the white memorial building, and wearing white uniforms, we were blinded most of the time. We had been refused permission to wear sunglasses, so instead of being able to read the music from our march cards, we had to play 'by ear'. After we had played the troops 'Onto Parade', Field Marshal Montgomery made his speech, which included the famous line "They gave their lives so that we might live". After inspecting the parade, the Field Marshal approached the Band.

"Good-morning, Bandmaster," he said.

"Good-morning, Sir," Waggie answered, standing stiffly to attention.

Field Marshal Montgomery walked along the lines, occasionally stopping to chat to one of the musicians. My heart nearly missed a beat when there, standing in front of me, stood 'Monty of Alamein'!

"How long have you been in the Royal Air Force, young man?" he asked me.

"Just under eighteen months, Sir," I replied, nervously.

"What is that strange little instrument you have there?" Monty enquired.

"It's a high reed instrument Sir, an Eb Clarinet," I enlightened him.

"Very interesting indeed," Monty said, then carried on to the end of the line.

"Thank you very much Flying Officer Wagner, very smart, very smart ... carry on."

"Thank you Sir," Waggie said, grinning like a Cheshire Cat.

I will always remember the War Graves; thousands upon thousands of stones lined up, reminding everyone present just how much human sacrifice had been made during the Second World War. The journey back to El Hamra passed uneventfully. 'Waggie' had given the Band the following day off, so I spent the best part of it in bed.

Our main form of recreation was swimming in the Bitter Lake, a section of the Suez Canal used by the armed forces for that purpose. One day during Siesta, Barry, a few others and I walked through Kasfahreet village, over the bridge which had the Sweet Water Canal running beneath it, then on to the Bitter Lake for a swim.

"You buy nice watch, Effendi?" a voice asked.

I turned to behold an Arab, with many watches strapped to his arms and wrists.

Barry tugged at my arm, "Come on lad, let's away," he warned.

"Don't be silly Barry," I retorted, "It won't hurt to look."

"Don't say I didn't warn thee," Barry went on, looking rather alarmed.

"I'll toss a coin and the winner, will take all, the price of the watch and the watch itself," the Arab offered.

"How much is the watch?" I asked."

"400 Ackers (£4)," came the eager reply.

"OK," I agreed, "But I will toss the coin and an independent person can hold the stakes."

I took a 2 piaster coin from my pocket and tossed it up into the air, caught it, then put it onto the back of my left hand, covering the coin with my right.

"Call," I said to the Arab.

"It is a head, Effendi," came the call.

I removed my right hand, to reveal a tail.

"Tails! You lose," I said excitedly.

"Please Effendi, I have a wife and ten children to support, please, please, toss the coin again."

"I warned thee," Barry whispered in my ear.

I wouldn't listen, I just turned to the Arab and said,

"I'll tell you what I will do, I'll toss the coin twice more and the best out of the three throws wins, is that alright?"

"Yes," the Arab agreed, "Thank you Effendi."

I flipped the coin twice more and it landed heads up, both times.

"That settles it!" I shouted triumphantly.

But I had spent so much time talking that I didn't see the Arab's next move. As quick as a flash, he whipped out a knife from under his jelabah and lunged at me. The flash of the blade made me jump back, but the sharp edge caught me across the bridge of my nose. Yet another scar to carry for the rest of my life.

The second of the Arabs, who had been holding the wagers, ran off and the first one scurried after him as fast as his legs would carry him.

"Stop! Thieves!" Barry shouted at the top of his voice.

Two Security Guards, armed with sten guns, rushed across the road, calling for the runaways to stop or they would fire! The villains paid no heed, but just kept on running. The guards called again, but were ignored. This time they fired warning shots over the Arabs' heads. 'Rat...a...tat...tat, they spluttered. The two men couldn't have wanted to live and, much to my horror, I saw them blown to pieces.

Even though my nose streamed with blood, I wouldn't have wished anyone to end his life like that. Barry scoffed at me for being so soft-hearted, as the Arabs would not have thought twice about killing me. All thoughts of swimming had disappeared from my mind; all I wished to do was lie down. Luckily for me, the Lido had its own Medical Officer, who, on inspecting my nose, assured me, "Although you will need stitches, you will be alright otherwise. You are a very lucky Bandsman."

"Yes Sir, I know," I replied.

I had to have twelve stitches in my nose.

That night, as I lay restlessly in my bed, I thought, 'I shall not be stopping to look at watches next time I go swimming, that's for sure!'

One of the highlights of the MEAF Band's ceremonial displays was the 'Beating of the Retreat' at dusk. Many military bands have performed this ceremony over the years, but it became twice as effective under floodlights in the desert. Our Band travelled thousands of miles, entertaining many servicemen and women and civilians with this famous display of music and marching. Each morning at 0700 the Band rehearsed its marching drill and music, striving for perfection. The line-up for the display was:

The Drum Major at the head of the columns

The front rank, consisting of three Trombones

Second rank: two Tubas and one Bass Trombone

Third: two French Horns and one Solo Cornet

Fourth: one Solo Cornet and two Second Cornets

Fifth: one Side Drum, one Bass Drum, one 3rd Cornet

Sixth: one Alto Sax, one 3rd Cornet, one Tenor Sax.

Seventh: one 3rd Clarinet, one 2nd Clarinet, one Oboe

Eighth: two Repiano Clarinets, one Solo Clarinet

Ninth: one Solo Clarinet, one Eb Clarinet Piccolo

The Bandmaster, bringing up the rear.

The Band lined up, facing front, in three ranks of nine, then the Drum Major took over the commands and the Dress Rehearsal began.

"Band, atten … tion!"

"Band, by the right, dress!"

"Band, eye…s front!"

"Band, into line in three columns of route… righ…t turn!"

The Drum Major took up his position at the head of the band and raised his Mace high above his head, vertically. As he brought it down directly in front of him, the band marched off, starting with the left foot, as per any normal marching procedure. After marching for five minutes, the Drum Major raised the Mace once more. The Drummers gave two lots of two sharp raps, followed by a three-beat drum roll, as a warning for the musicians to look up. The Mace came down again and two three-beat rolls were the signal to start playing 'The Royal Air Force March', our first piece, during which the counter-march took place.

The Band continued playing whilst performing that manoeuvre. The Mace was raised vertically yet again and this time the trombonists in the front rank raised their instruments as a signal that the counter-march would soon take place. At the same time came the warning procedure by the drummers. The Drum Major, holding out his right arm, stretched the Mace out horizontally and performed a 'U' turn, marching through the three columns towards the rear of the band. The trombonists followed suit, then each rank did likewise. Finally, the Bandmaster followed through, until the band faced the opposite way to how it had commenced.

After a few more manoeuvres the band came to a halt. The Grand Finale would soon take place; the pieces of music being 'Nimrod', 'Sunset' and 'the Last Post'. After a short sermon by the Camp Padre the reveille sounded to end the performance.

Days at El Hamra were becoming more and more hectic. With the Beating of the Retreat rehearsals, studying for promotional exams and giving concerts, I barely knew whether I was coming or going. Although the intense heat certainly sapped our energy, the afternoon swim became a 'must'. My nose healed and I did my best to forget the incident at the Bitter Lake. On one of those hot, humid days, I decided to go for a swim on my own. Barry had a lot of studying to catch up on and none of the others could be bothered, so I gathered my things together and headed for the 'Lido'. I stopped on the bridge and looked down at the 'Sweet Water Canal'. 'What a stupid name to call it', I thought. The name canal was a joke in itself, as it wasn't wide or deep enough to carry vessels of any description, let alone barges. As for the water being sweet – it certainly didn't look it! Nevertheless, the villagers of Kasfahreet used it for laundering, drinking and anything else water could be used for. I couldn't understand how they weren't all riddled with disease. The term 'Arabs' as loosely used by the Western World could hardly have been applicable to these people. Even the description 'peasants' would have seemed generous, as they were quite nondescript.

After watching the women washing their clothes and children playing in the filthy water (ugh!) I sauntered along the dusty, makeshift road, trying not to look at the butchers shops where the meat hung outside, covered with flies.

At last, I reached the Bitter Lake Lido, paid my entrance fee of 5 piasters and went into the water. Even though the sun felt scorching hot, the water seemed chilly. I shivered and splashed around to keep warm.

It was there, in the Bitter Lake, that I met Andreana Kyriakou, daughter of millionaire bus company magnate Efthasios Kyriakou, who had the Public Transport monopoly in Cyprus. The Kyriakous were Greek Cypriots and were just spending a couple of days with their friend, Colonel Bill Smethers who, despite being CO of the KOYLIs, loved sailing. He rented a villa at Ismaelia, some ten miles or so away, although how he managed it on army pay mystified me. Rumour had it that Colonel Bill's dad was a financier in the City of London.

I soon would have an experience that, by way of a change, would be a pleasant one. I had been swimming about for a while when I saw her standing there. How was it possible, that there, in the middle of nowhere, could be such a beautiful girl? Her skin was dark but not too much so, her hair black, cut short with a fringe at the front. We sat on the sand, talking for a while, letting the sea wash over our feet. Andreana's English left quite a bit to be desired, but I managed to understand her, at least, most of the time.

"We are going for a trip later on this afternoon, on Uncle Bill's power-boat 'Flying Fish'. Would you like to come?" Andreana asked.

"I don't think that your Uncle or your Father, would like that," I answered.

"I will ask them," she continued, "And by the way, Bill is not my real Uncle, just a friend of Daddy's.

With that she stood up and ran over to where Efthasios and Bill, were sitting sipping their 'Stella' beer. I watched them and wondered, what were they saying. After a few moments Andreana ran back to me, laughing excitedly and shouting, "You can come, Peter!" I couldn't believe it. I had always wanted to sail in a power-boat and now my dream would soon come true.

"I will have to be back at camp before midnight," I told her.

"Don't worry, Uncle Bill will make sure that you have," Andreana assured me.

"Will," I corrected her.

"Will what?" she looked at me quizzically.

"Uncle Bill will make sure, that I 'will' be back in time, not 'have'," I explained.

"Oh dear, I am sorry," she continued, "I have not got, the good English."

I laughed and said, "Don't worry , I will help you."

The 'Flying Fish' skimmed across the water at a breath-taking speed and both Andreana and I stood together, holding onto the safety rail, feeling slightly nervous, yet excited. Bill had provided us with waterproofs, so we would stay reasonably dry, even though the waves were washing over the bow.

"I should have joined the Navy, instead of the Royal Air Force!" I shouted, trying to make myself heard above the noise of the engine and the sea.

Andreana just laughed, because she couldn't hear a thing I said, even though I screamed and shouted.

The trip on the 'Flying Fish' had lasted for four hours and, to put the finishing touch to a perfect day, Efthasios flew me back to camp in his private helicopter. I thanked the three of them for a perfect day and said to Andreana, "I hope we will meet again, perhaps in Cyprus, when the band is transferred there, next year."

"I do hope so," she replied sadly, wishing that she could see me again.

The weeks that followed were not as hectic as the previous ones had been, so other members of the Band and I found ourselves with quite a lot of free time on our hands. There were, of course, rehearsals and individual practice, but even so, apart from swimming, there wasn't an awful lot to do.

The No.6 Regional Band had been in Egypt for six months and I, along with the other musicians, now felt homesick. Not that I missed my home that much, but I certainly missed things like dancing or popping into the 'Spotted Dog' pub at Neasden for a pint or two. I also missed the English girls.

One day, Cpl Bob Pullen and 'bumper-up' solo clarinet player Malcolm (Mouse) Simmonds were playing five card draw poker in Bob's tent. Brian and I were talking outside, when Bob called out.

"Hey you two… fancy a game of Brag?"

"That's a good idea," Brian replied, "How about you Peter?"

"No thanks," I said, "I've never played. Besides I can't afford to gamble."

"We'll only be playing for two acker stakes. That won't break you, will it?" Brian said jokingly.

"Oh all right," I submitted, laughing, "But you will have to show me how to play first."

Bob, 'Mouse' and Brian played a few 'dummy' hands with me so that I would know how to play the game, at least.

"It's quite an easy game," I said. 'More luck than judgement' is what I really thought. That's where I made my first mistake! 'Mouse' dealt out five cards, face downwards, to each player, then the same amount to himself. I looked at my cards; the six of clubs, the king of clubs, king of hearts, three of diamonds and the seven of spades.

'Mouse' had dealt to me first, so he asked, "How many cards, do you want to exchange?"

"Three please," I answered. I hoped to get either one more king, making a prial of kings, or two more, making four of a kind, which is one of the top hands.

'Mouse' took the discards and put them at the bottom of the pack. Next he dealt three others, from the top. He repeated the question to Bob, who exchanged one card, then to Brian who wanted two, and after that 'Mouse' had to exchange his own cards.

"I won't change any," he said.

"Oh-oh!" Bob joked, "Our 'Mousie' has got a sitter! It must be at the least a run."

"I'm saying nothing," Mouse remarked, with a poker-face.

"He could be bluffing," Brian teased.

"I doubt it, knowing our Mouse," Bob laughed.

I started to think, 'Brian asked for two cards, so he must have had a prial dealt to him. Bob wanted one, so he must have had two pairs, I wonder...' I looked at my cards and observed that I now had four kings, four of a kind! The hand could only be beaten by four aces, four fours or a Royal Flush (the Americans call it an 'inside straight'). That hand is virtually impossible to attain, so I could gamble with comparative safety. I wagered 10 piasters and immediately, Bob stacked his cards.

"That hand is too good for me," he moaned.

"What did you have?" I asked.

"You'll have to pay me, if you want to see," Bob replied.

"That's the rules," Brian spoke up.

"Oh, sorry, I didn't realise," I apologised.

Brian sat for a while, then said, "I'll see your 10 piasters, and raise you another 20."

I didn't like that at all.

"I thought we were only playing for two ackers a game," I grumbled.

"Who opened with a bet of ten ackers then?" Brian demanded, argumentatively.

'Mouse's turn came at last.

"I'll see your thirty, Brian, and raise you another forty."

I didn't realise it at the time, but 'Mouse' bluffed all of the time, and thought he could bluff me out of the game. I thought for a moment, then remembered that I must have the third top hand possible, and continued ...

"I will see your 70 ackers and raise you a further 100. That makes it 170 ackers for you to bet, Brian."

By that time my nerve had started to give way, and it showed on my face. Brian looked at me, then raised the bet to 500 ackers. 'Mouse' had thrown in his cards by that time, then I suddenly realised, that 'Mouse' had been bluffing! An awful thought suddenly came into my head, 'Could they have been playing together?' I told myself off, 'Don't be ridiculous; it's only a silly game'.

"This has become ludicrous, for a friendly game," I said to Brian, "So I will see you for £5."

Brian confidently turned over his cards, to reveal four queens.

"That was an expensive game for you, Pete!" he said, with a laugh, ready to pick up the 'kitty'.

"Not so fast Brian," I snapped. "Four kings certainly beats four queens!"

"If I had landed a hand like that, I would have played until I dropped," Brian said, sarcastically.

"It's just as well for you, then, that I haven't got your nerve, isn't it Brian?" I answered finally.

In spite of winning, I wished I had never been talked into playing that game of poker, and promised myself, that I wouldn't be drawn into another one.

Christmas would soon be upon us and the band would have to fly to RAF Nicosia, Cyprus to 'Beat the Retreat', play for a VIP parade and give a military band concert. The musicians were going to be in Cyprus for one week, then we would be returning to Egypt in time for Christmas. The week spent in Cyprus, although extremely busy, cheered us up. It made a pleasant change to sleep in a billet instead of a tent. After settling in, Harry Whipps issued the musicians with a pass each, so that we could go into Nicosia to do some sight-seeing.

"You will have to wear 'civvies'," he told us. "We are still under 'Emergency Regulations', so be careful, lads. In Egypt, we are always at risk, but here it's even worse, so be on your guard at all times and stick together, OK?"

"Right Sarge," everyone agreed.

Cpl Bob, Barry, four others and I waited for the bus that would take us into Nicosia. When it arrived, I looked at the name on the side of it, 'Efthasios Kyriakou'. I wished I had Andreana's address, but I didn't, so I could not go to see her. The bus dropped the musicians off in Ledra Street, the main high street of Nicosia and we were pleasantly surprised to see modern shops. In Egypt there were mainly stalls and goods being sold by the wayside, but very few shops. I must have been different in Cairo or Alexandria, but the band hadn't been to either of those places at that time. After buying a few souvenirs we were feeling thirsty.

"Let's have a beer," I suggested.

"Good idea," the others agreed.

There were plenty of bars in Nicosia, but remembering Sgt Whipps warning, we were extremely careful.

"This bar looks OK to me," Bob remarked, so in we all went.

We sat down on the stools at the bar.

"I notice there is no draught beer," Brian said, a look of disappointment on his face.

"What do you expect?" I retorted, "You know there's no draught in this part of the world!"

"Oh what I wouldn't give for a lovely cool pint of bitter," Bob said, drooling at the thought of it.

"Seven bottles of 'Keo' beer please," Bob ordered, "and seven glasses of 'ouzo' (aniseed).

The Armenian girl behind the counter laughed.

"You lot will get drunk," she scolded.

"That's the idea," we all answered.

"I see that you've been shopping," she said, in her broken English. "Presents for wives, or sweethearts?" she enquired.

"We are not married," Bob answered indignantly.

"Even sweethearts are out of the question," I added.

"Why is that?" she asked with a look of amazement on her face.

"Look at the life that we lead." Mouse had spoken up for the first time.

The musicians returned to camp, none the worse for our few drinks, in fact it had been a break, seeing a bit of civilization for a change. As we neared the billet I saw something.

"What's that on the wall," I said.

"It's a chameleon," Bob answered "Look, it changing colour to blend in with the wall," Brian remarked.

"It is a well known fact that chameleons change colour to whatever background they are on," Bob explained.

"I wonder what would happen if we put it on a Scottish Tartan?" I laughed.

"It would die, stupid," Barry replied.

"Ask a stupid question, get a stupid answer," I concluded.

The following morning the band had a rehearsal with the Squadron of RAF Nicosia for a parade to honour the visit of the 'Secretary of State for Air'. The heat made it almost impossible to breathe, the thermometer reading over 100 degrees Fahrenheit, but at least a slight breeze blew in from the Mediterranean. The Squadron made a success of the parade and 'Waggie' gave us the afternoon off, to enable us to prepare ourselves for the evening concert in the camp cinema.

The Astra cinema had filled to capacity, as it had been some months since the Squadron had seen a live performance. The No. 6 Regional Band took its place on the stage and then the Bandmaster made his entrance. Waggie strutted onto the stage like a peacock, Sgt Whipps called the Band to attention, and as the musicians stood up, rapturous applause erupted. The Bandmaster raised his baton and each of us musicians brought up our own instrument to the ready position in complete synchronisation. That alone brought cheers and applause from the audience.

After playing the 'Royal Air Force March' we played the 'Planets Suite' by Gustav Holtz. The audience appreciated the latter, but the next medley of tunes nearly 'brought the house down'. It was a special arrangement of Glen Miller numbers and although military, rather than dance band style, it really went down a treat. 'Moonlight Serenade' was followed by 'Little Brown Jug', 'Pensylvania 65000', 'Tuxedo Junction' and a reprise of 'Moonlight Serenade' to finish.

The 'New World Symphony' by Dvorak ended the performance and by this time the MEAF Band had really been taken into everyone's hearts. As we marched off playing the RAF March, we were clapped so much it looked as if we were never going to be allowed to leave the cinema.

The week in Cyprus passed by successfully and No.6 Regional Band returned to Egypt. I had bought a couple of bottles of Ouzo and some bottled Keo beer, and every member of the band had similarly brought some drink with them, it being easier to obtain in Cyprus than in Egypt. Christmas that year would turn out to be quite an event!

I don't remember too much about Christmas 1954 in Egypt, except that I awoke on Christmas Day, lying in the sun, sprawled out on the sand with an empty Ouzo bottle in my hand. I looked around to see bodies everywhere. They weren't dead, just members of the band, having enjoyed a great Christmas, and just sleeping it off!

By 1955 the trouble in the Canal Zone had eased off considerably, but in Cyprus EOKA and ENOSIS terrorists were attacking military installations. The problems in Cyprus went back 200 years to the historic 'Battle of Attaturk Square', where thousands of Turks were slaughtered by the Greeks. These two communities still hate one another to this day, but with a United Nations peacekeeping force, there is not nearly as much friction. For that same reason, British troops were in Cyprus in the 1950s.

No.6 Regional Band MEAF were transferred to Cyprus and would be stationed at RAF Episkopi. The camp spread out over a wide area on the side of a range of hills, close to the Mediterranean Sea. The band's living quarters were yet again (ugh!) tents, though not so close to each other as at El Hamra. The climate in Cyprus felt much more pleasant than Egypt. Although the heat had the same intensity, the Mediterranean breezes made it much easier to bear.

Over the years, goats had made a track leading down the side of the cliffs from the camp to the beach. When the lads wished to have a swim, we had to walk, or should I say scramble, down it. Once the Band had settled in at Episkopi, we soon eased into a routine and toured around more often than we had before.

St Hilarion Castle had been used for the filming of the original Walt Disney Snow White and the seven Dwarfs and created an amazing spectacle! Situated high in the Kyrenian Hills, the castle was, and I assume still is, a tourist paradise. The band, including myself, managed to have a look around other places of interest during our stay in Cyprus. Of course, this could only be done when there had been a lull in terrorist activities. Mount Troudos had become another interesting feature of Cyprus and my companions and I used to picnic at the foot of it.

After two weeks the band went on tour again, first to RAF Habbaniya in Iraq, one of our more hazardous exploits. We travelled on a RAF Hastings four-engined plane and landed, in intense heat, at 0230 hours. The atmosphere felt quite humid, even at that time of night. No sooner had we been shown to our billet when we heard an enormous explosion. Apparently an aeroplane carrying troops, en-route to England, had exploded on take-off. Later that morning, after rising and going to the mess for breakfast, my friends and I made conversation with two Air-Sea-Rescue crewmembers. The story they related horrified us. An RAF Hastings had, as previously mentioned, exploded on take-off, tragically killing 125 servicemen and their families. The poor fellows were sick to their stomachs at the task they had to perform. I will not enlarge on the gruesome details, but sabotage was suspected, although it would be a long time before that could be proven.

The following day, some of my fellow musicians an I took taxis into Baghdad and, after a rough journey, were dropped off in Rashid Street. There wasn't a lot to see in Baghdad, but we were always interested to see new places. We visited the

Forces Club, the only place not 'out of bounds' to the Armed Forces. After a few drinks we were approached by an Arab.

"Want to have a nice time, Effendis?" he asked us.

Barry and I weren't too keen, but were soon persuaded by the others. By this time it had reached 0900 hours, not exactly the time for sight-seeing. The taxi dropped us off outside a house where there were girls leaning out of the windows.

"Come inside, English gentlemen," they called.

"Let's go in, just for a laugh," Brian suggested.

"I don't know about that..." I answered, warily. "It's out of bounds and we could all land up in the 'glasshouse'.

As there were twelve of us, we considered that there would be 'safety in numbers', so after dismissing the taxi, we went into the house. We were met by girls of various nationalities, Arabic, French, Italian, African and even an English girl. After having a laugh and a joke, Bob said, "Let's go lads, that's enough."

We all agreed, but it wasn't as easy as all that...

"What's your game?" the 'Madam' of the establishment said, angrily. "This is a business. Doesn't anyone want to take advantage of our hospitality?" By this time, four extremely nasty looking Arabs had walked into the room.

"We had better scarper, and quick!" I said, feeling quite nervous.

Bob took the initiative by rushing out of the room and the rest of us quickly followed suit. As we rushed out of the house and down a side street back onto the main road, I spotted a jeep containing two MPs.

"Look out, the Redcaps!" I warned them. Luckily the cops seemed to be pre-occupied and didn't appear to notice the commotion.

Back at RAF Habbaniya we were discussing the events of the previous day when Sgt Whipps called the band to rehearsal.

"Come on lads," he said. "We have a show to give tonight in the Camp Theatre."

Before the performance that evening, some of the lads and I decided to have a drink in the NAAFI. Unfortunately, one drink led to another and I could hardly see the music by the time it came to play! To make matters worse, I had a solo to play in 'Orpheus in the Underworld', the oboist having been recalled to England on compassionate grounds, so the Eb clarinet had to play the solo. The Bandmaster pointed his baton at me, my cue to play, but as I attempted to stand up, I fell over, taking my music stand and all the music with me! Luckily the audience, including the Camp CO, thought we were performing a comedy routine. 'Waggie' looked furious, but accepted my explanation that it was an accident.

The third day in Iraq we performed in Baghdad, at the Alawiyah Club, a place mainly for high-ranking civilians, such as Sheiks, Ministers and Royalty. The only other people allowed in there were Officers of Her Majesty's Forces. Even they were only allowed entry by invitation. The performance went well and afterwards we were treated to a meal, followed by a refreshing ice-cold beer to round it off! On our way back to camp I looked out of the coach window and noticed a large crowd in the Market Square, shouting and cheering.

"What's all that commotion over there?" I asked the driver.

"It is a thief, having his hand cut off," the Bedouin guide answered.

I nearly choked on the slice of orange I had in my mouth.

"Pardon?" I exclaimed.

The guide repeated himself, then explained that if a thief was apprehended, the custom still existed to cut off a limb.

"I should think that there is hardly any crime in Baghdad, then," I said, feeling a little sick.

"That is the most surprising part of it," the Bedouin answered, sadly. "Even though this severe penalty still exists, there is a high theft rate here in Baghdad."

As the coach started to climb a small hill, we heard a splutter and a bang, then it came to an abrupt halt. After spending a quarter of an hour under the bonnet, the driver shrugged his shoulders and said, "It's no use, you'll all have to get out and push."

What an amusing sight to see all those musicians pushing the coach. Luckily for us, an army lorry passing by, stopped, and we were able to hop into it, leaving the coach to be collected later. While the lorry remained stationary at the traffic-lights, a group of Bedouin horsemen came galloping past us and, much to our surprise, jumped their horses over cars and lorries. That must have been the most amazing spectacle I had ever witnessed, even more breathtaking than 'Zag-a-Zig' railway station. I wished I had brought my camera with me.

Another visit that would forever stand out in my memory was to the Iraq Petroleum Company. The band had been transported in a Bristol Freighter, which had to be the noisiest and the most uncomfortable aircraft we had had the misfortune to fly in to date. As the plane taxied along the runway it backfired, just like an 'old banger'. The plane flew us to a small airstrip a few miles from our destination, then we musicians were transferred to 'doves' – small, single-engined planes owned by the oil company. On arrival we were met by officials of the Iraq Petroleum Co. We were then split up into groups of two. I would be lodging with a charming couple, Jack, his wife Anne, and their two children, Rose and June. The family originated in Manchester, so I knew many of the places they spoke of.

"I expect you are both hungry after your flight," Jane said, "How would you like a nice salad?"

Barry and I both looked at each other, then replied, "That would be lovely, thank you."

I felt a little surprised, "How do you manage to grow salad in the desert?" I asked.

"Come into the back garden and I'll show you," June answered.

We both followed her and were pleasantly surprised to see a flourishing garden. It had quite an assortment of things that one would expect to find at home in England.

"Didn't you know that sand is the most fertile soil in the world, once it has been irrigated?" Jack asked us.

"You could have fooled me," Barry answered laughing.

The Iraq Petroleum Sports and Social Club had the reputation of being 'out of this World' to coin a phrase! It had cost £1,000,000 to build and we had never seen anything like it, not even in England. The building had everything, from two swimming pools and tennis courts, to a spacious restaurant with large ballroom. More like a luxury hotel than a social club.

That evening the Military Band set up outside on the veranda of the club, ready for our performance. We were exceptionally well received and were given drinks before starting to play. The sky twinkling with thousands of stars turned it into a beautiful evening, with the 'Milky Way' prominent and 'Great Bear' clear to see, even to the naked eye. The No.6 Regional Band commenced their performance, in the usual way, with the RAF March. After playing a few marches, one of the company directors came up to 'Waggie'.

"Would it be possible," he requested, "For me to conduct the Band, Mr Wagner?"

"Certainly Sir," Waggie replied, smiling and winking at us musicians.

"I have always wanted to conduct a band playing my favourite piece of music, 'Little Brown Jug'," the gentleman said, "Is that possible?"

The Bandmaster passed the baton to him, then stood behind the man, ready to take over, in the unlikely event of him breaking down. Although not a professional, the company director coped quite well with the conducting, and when he had finished the entire Band applauded him.

After the Military Band performance, the Dance Band took over, thus leaving a few of the musicians who were not playing, to enjoy themselves.

"The Military Band sounded wonderful," the organiser's wife admitted, but the Dance Band is even better, it really is exciting."

On that particular occasion I did not play with the Dance Band, so I joined in with the dancing, and at times helped out with the Master of Ceremonies' job. By the time the evening had drawn to a close, after so much to eat and drink, Barry and I were full, almost to bursting, and the following day there were quite a few 'hangovers' in No.6 Regional Band ... including mine! As the plane carrying the band took off I remarked: "From the way the plane's rolling around, I reckon the pilot must have had too much to drink last night as well!" The others agreed with me.

After an extremely hectic two days, the band returned to our base at RAF Episkopi. There were parades, concerts and Officers' Mess dinners to play for, and during the next few weeks the band remained in Cyprus.

The terrorists had stepped up their campaign to remove British troops from Cyprus and, on one or two occasions, we No.6 Regional bandsmen had narrow escapes with our lives.

One night Barry, the rest of the band and I were sleeping peacefully in our tents when suddenly we heard a loud explosion, then another, followed by many more, scaring the life out of us.

I leapt out of bed.

"What on earth was that, Barry?" I shouted nervously.

"It sounded like bombs to me," my friend answered.

We grabbed our rifles and dashed out of the tent. At least six of the tents had been blown up. Luckily for us, the bandsmen's tents had escaped the bombers, but in the next compound they had borne the brunt of the terrorist attack. Unfortunately for the servicemen of RAF Episkopi, due to the campsite being spread out over the hillside, it was extremely vulnerable. Each time the Band left the camp, we had to travel in specially reinforced coaches with iron bars on the windows, accompanied by armed guards.

The next tour would take us to Tobruk, Tripoli and Aden and we would be away for one month. At the first port of call, Tobruk, after being shown to our billets we proceeded to wash and change into civilian clothes. Barry took out his toothbrush to clean his teeth and could not believe what he could taste. Salt water actually ran from the tap! Of all the things that had happened to us, that took some believing! Someone had forgotten to inform us that all the drinking water had to be boiled before use. Fortunately, that did not apply to the mess, where the drinking water had been treated to remove the salt.

Of all the places we visited, the town of Tobruk had received the worst wartime battering, the Salvation Army HQ being the only building left standing, but as we would only be spending a couple of days there, it didn't really matter.

We had loaded up the Hastings aircraft and boarded it at 0730, en-route for Tripoli. As we settled back into our seats

Brian suggested a game of cards, but I declined, keeping my promise to myself, despite the fact that there always seemed to be a game going on somewhere or the other.

I fastened ready for the take-off and on looking out of the porthole, suddenly became aware of a trail of smoke coming from one of the engines.

"Look at that, Barry!" I exclaimed. "We're on fire!"

"It's nothing," my friend replied, confidently. "This plane has automatic fire extinguishers built into the engines that are set off if they overheat."

That may well have been the case, but the next thing to happen did not inspire confidence, because the engine suddenly burst into flames! Luckily, fire tenders were quickly on the scene and soon had the fire under control, using foam. There was a delay of some two hours while the engineers checked over the engine and when they were perfectly satisfied that the plane could proceed safely on its journey, we took off.

RAF Idris in Tripoli had the reputation of being the best camp in the Middle East, and we most certainly agreed. The Band Block, not unlike RAF Uxbridge, housed three to a room. The beds were more modern than the lads had previously experienced, and the food certainly pleased the palate. We were in for ten days of living almost like civilians. Not only were we told to wear civilian clothes when we left the camp but 'Waggie' also allowed us to rehearse in 'civvies', the only instances when we were obliged to wear uniform being parades, concerts or ceremonial displays.

After a good night's rest we got up, had breakfast and went to the rehearsal room. Sergeant Harry Whipps would be taking practice that morning, so he chased everybody up.

"Get fell in!" he shouted, in his familiar Geordie accent.

"Harry?" Bob asked, "Isn't it about time we had a change of programme? The lads are becoming bored with the same old pieces of music, and so am I?"

Harry looked at Bob for a moment before answering.

"You know what 'Waggie' is like," he said, "he doesn't like to try out new things."

"But surely he would listen to you, wouldn't he?" Bob suggested.

"I'll try... but I don't think I'll have much luck," said Harry, cautiously, but after running through a few marches he said, "Right lads, let's try something different this morning, and perhaps when the Bandmaster hears it, he might decide for himself that it's a good idea."

"That's crafty," Bob agreed.

The first piece was 'Waltzing Clarinets', featuring the clarinet section.

"If you remain standing all the way through the number," Harry told us, then sway from side to side during the main theme, it will be most effective."

As predicted, Waltzing Clarinets went like a dream. 'Waggie' came into the room half-way through the piece and looked noticeably impressed.

"I think it's about time," he suggested, "we incorporated some show pieces into our programme."

Harry winked at Bob and whispered "See what I mean?"

Bob had to agree, and from then on the Military Band programmes were far more interesting, for the musicians as well as the audiences.

Tripoli had a beauty that was quite unlike anywhere else that we had vitited. It reminded me more of the Bahamas, with Palm Trees lining the Promenade and busy shopping precincts, buzzing with people. A few of my friends and I went sight-seeing and it made a pleasant change not to have Arabs or beggars pestering us at every street corner.

Language was the main problem for non-Italian speaking people visiting Tripoli. The members of the band had learned to speak some Arabic, a little Greek and even some Turkish, but even though nearly all musical terms and abbreviations are expressed in Italian, it didn't make any of us fluent in the language.

"I spoke to some of the medics yesterday," Bob said to the others, "Apparently, there is a casino here in Tripoli."

Barry spoke up next. "Let's ask the policeman on traffic-duty, he'll know where it is."

"Good idea," came the unanimous reply.

Bob picked his way through the busy traffic until he arrived at the podium, from which the policeman directed the bustling traffic.

"Excuse me," he asked, "Where is the Casino?"

"*Non capisco Inglese!*" the man answered, abruptly.

"If he doesn't understand English," Barry said, "How does he know that you were speaking it?"

"He doesn't *want* to understand," Mouse joined in.

The four of us carried on walking until we saw a building with a sign displaying 'Casino'. We went up the steps and were confronted by two extremely large 'bouncers'.

"Members only," they said, gruffly.

"Can't we pay to go in?" Barry asked.

The bouncers looked at one another and laughed.

"English servicemen cannot afford twenty dinars, I am sure," the taller of the two said.

"Twenty quid! He's right," Bob agreed, "Let's go chaps."

The Saturday-night dance at RAF Idris had become a regular weekly affair, but this particular one would be different. The Camp CO had asked 'Waggie' if he could supply a dance band, so the Bandmaster requested volunteers. We already had an established showband in our group, but only a small group had been requested on that occasion. The line-up chosen was as follows: Myself on Alto Sax/Clt, Bob Pullen on Trombone, Tony playing String-Bass, plus the Camp Pianist to complete the ensemble. The Cookhouse had been chosen to be the venue, but after it had been decorated with streamers and balloons, you wouldn't have recognised it as such. In addition to playing with the Band I would be standing in as the MC. I had previous experience when running my own band. The evening began in grand style, with the Hall soon filling up with people intent on enjoying themselves.

During the interval there were records to dance to, so inevitably I asked a young girl to dance with me. During the course of the conversation, I discovered that she was an American Radar Officer, stationed at USAF Wheelus Field not to far from us. She thought the band sounded fabulous, and told me so. Finally, the music for that particular set of dances, came to an end, and as we approached the table, Rebecca introduced me to her two companions, Hank and Chuck. They too were Radar Officers, and the four of us had a pleasant chat. The evening had been a great success, and after having coffee with my new-found friends, Rebecca invited me to visit her at USAF Wheelus Field. As there were not any emergency restrictions in Tripoli, I would be able to go out alone, not even needing a special pass.

The Beating of the Retreat Ceremony would be taking place on the seafront in Tripoli and as we were going to perform some new movements, so the musicians had to spend a considerable amount of time 'on the square'. The lads had lined up in our usual formation, three ranks of nine facing to the front. Harry Whipps, in his role as Drum Major, took up his position facing the Band.

"Band, atten...tion!" he ordered. "Band, into line in three columns of route, righ...t turn!" Next Harry marched smartly to the head of the band, then stamped sharply to attention, facing it.

"OK lads," he said, "Let's get the dressing sorted out."

With that, he paced out the distance between each rank, then each column. One... two... three... halt, the Drum Major marched and stopped.

"Get into line there, Bass Drummer," he ordered.

Finally, satisfied that there were three paces between each rank, then each column, the Drum Major proceeded with the rehearsal. Harry performed a smart 'about turn' on the spot, then raised his mace, the signal for 'marching on the spot'. Left, right, left, right, left... Two double taps on the side drum and bass drum, gave the warning for the musicians to look up. The mace came down, signalling the band to march off at normal 'quick march' tempo.

As the band marched along, the side drummer performed a rhythmic solo, then afterwards gave two double warning taps and a drum roll. That signalled the band to raise instruments, ready to commence playing. The Drum Major lifted the mace high into the air, to enable the musicians to see it. Next, the two three-beat rolls, and the 'RAF March' started the medley of tunes.

The next movement was the counter-march. The Drum Major signalled in the usual way and the Trombonists raised their instruments. Two double taps on the drums, then the movement commenced. After the counter-march, two double taps, then one three-beat roll, the signal to change the music. All this happened while the musicians were in motion. For the next movement, a slow march 'Scipio' had to be inserted into the cardholders. The signal was given to change step from quick to slow march and while the slow march continued, the Drum Major gave a display with the mace, twirling it around clockwise, then anti-clockwise, tossing it high into the air. The audience that had gathered quickly, watched expectantly, perhaps waiting for Harry to drop it as it came hurtling down again; but if that is what they were hoping to see, they would surely be disappointed. The Drum Major caught the mace with the expertise one would expect of a professional in the Royal Air Force. After further aerobatics with the mace, he held it vertically again for the band to see. The drummers gave their usual signal, for the musicians to stop playing. Now the musicians were marching, with their instruments at the 'carry' position: clarinets, piccolo, cornets, trombones (all with instruments held, in the left hand), bass (tuba), saxes, bass drum (all attached by slings/straps and held in front), side drums attached by a strap and held at the side. After the marching display came the Finale, which included the pieces of music Nimrod, Sunset, the Last Post and Reveille, then the Padre's prayer to finish.

At last the time had arrived for my visit to USAF Wheelus Field and I felt quite excited. Hank arrived in a staff car at 1400 hrs to take me to the base. As the vehicle drew up outside the Band Block, Bob called out to me.

"Hey, Your Majesty, your carriage awaits."

"Clever clogs!" I answered, laughing.

"Anyone would think, that you were about to visit King Faizal, toffed up like that," Barry teased.

"That's right," I joked, "Didn't you know? See you later lads."

As I clambered into the camouflaged, six-door limousine, standing there waiting for me, I felt terribly important.

"Hi there Pete," Hank drawled in his Texan accent.

"Good afternoon Hank," I replied, as the staff car whisked us away.

As we approached, I stared at the camp surrounds. Considering that no conflict existed in Tripoli, the Base looked like a fortress. It had a high barbed-wire fence around it, with a sign warning that the wire had been electrified. We were stopped at the main gate, by an armed guard. As he saluted (quite smartly, for a Yank, I thought) he asked Hank for some means of identification.

"This is my guest Musician Bradbury," Hank informed the Sergeant, as he showed the ID card to him.

"Carry on gentlemen," the sentry answered, acknowledging me, then saluting once more.

"I cannot believe this, Hank," I said. "I don't have any rank, but I am being treated like a VIP."

Hank smiled at me. "Maybe you don't Pete," he said, "But I have, and you are my guest, which means that you will be treated as such."

Hank certainly wasn't joking, as I soon found out.

Rebecca and Chuck met us outside the Officers' Club and we were about to go inside when I whispered to Rebecca, "I cannot go in there, I'm not an officer."

"You are our guest Peter," she answered, "And will be given the same courtesy as ourselves, just behave as if you belong here, OK?"

From that moment on, life seemed like a dream to me. Rebecca held onto my arm, steering me into the enormous dining-hall. Luckily for me I had pressed my best suit, polished my shoes and put on my black 'dickie-bow'. Most of the Americans were in dress uniform, but Rebecca and her two colleagues had donned civilian clothes, so that I would not feel out of place. I had been introduced to many people, but when Rebecca introduced me to the CO of the base, I couldn't help but marvel at the way that they put me at ease!

"Hi there, Pete," the Commanding Officer greeted me, shaking my hand, "I hear that you are a great jazz musician."

"I wouldn't say that Sir, not by any stretch of the imagination!" I replied modestly.

"Not so much of the 'sir', just call me Arnie," the CO continued, "You are a guest, here at my base!"

We all sat down to dinner, with the CO at the head of the long, candle-lit table. I had been placed in between Rebecca and Hank, so that I wouldn't feel too conspicuous. The meal was delicious; I chose veal cutlets with roast potatoes. After the meal, which had included champagne, I felt tired enough to fall asleep, but of course, on that special day, I certainly made sure that I did not!

"How would you fancy a stroll around the PX store, Peter?" Rebecca asked.

"What's that?" I enquired, feeling a trifle stupid at not knowing.

"It's the equivalent of your NAAFI," Chuck spoke up, for the first time.

"We thought you had lost your voice, which is most unusual for you," Rebecca and Hank both echoed.

"Sorry y'all," Chuck drawled, "I've been a bit seedy today!"

When we arrived, I stared in absolute amazement.

"Well..." I said, "If the PX is the equivalent of the NAAFI, I'll be a monkey's uncle!"

There were cars, washing machines and virtually everything that one could wish to buy. I felt dumbfounded.

"The largest thing you can buy in the NAAFI is a crate of beer," I remarked.

My friends laughed at that, and as we carried on walking around the colossal store, I spotted my favourite cigarettes, Pall Mall King Size, with roasted tobacco, made in the USA, of course! I loved a long cool smoke in those days. Hank made a present of 200 to me, to take back.

After the visit to the PX, the four of us went on a tour of the base, so could see as much as possible in the short time I would be staying there. There were, of course, restricted areas, but my companions made sure that I saw as much as I was permitted to.

As we approached the 'square' we observed a military band being put through its paces. I noticed a vast difference between that band and the No. 6 Regional. For one thing, they wore a white cravat, belt and gaiters, with a white top-cover over their peaked caps. They wore a similar Best Blue uniform to the one worn by ourselves, in the UK. For another, their marching did not appear to be as stiff, nor as starchy as the British military bands (actually, I thought they looked sloppy, but did not want to hurt their feelings by saying so). The band played my favourite kind of music: 'Big Band Jazz' on the march, and that really did give me a thrill – St Louis Blues, Chattanooga Choo–Choo, Pensylvania 65000, to name but a few of Glen Miller's Big Band tunes.

"What did you think of that, Peter?" Rebecca asked.

"The music sounded great," I answered her, "But I do prefer our way of marching, I must admit."

"We have to agree with you there," my three friends said, in unison.

After an evening of dancing to records and drinking in the Officers' Club, I had to say farewell to USAF Wheelus Field. My friends reluctantly, took me back to RAF Idris, and I even more reluctantly, bid them farewell.

Due to problems in Aden, the Band's visit there, had to be postponed, and the musicians were obliged to return to RAF Episkopi. It had been an exciting tour and my fellow musicians and I were not at all pleased to return to the trouble-torn island.

The following few weeks were full of tragedy for me. First of all, my Grandfather died, soon to be followed by my Grandma, then to top it all, Uncle Walt died also. I applied for compassionate leave, but could hardly believe it when the 'Powers that Be' turned me down. I had been able to understand having been refused leave to go to Ruth's wedding, but losing both my grandparents and Uncle Walt, all within a short while of one another, then being refused compassionate leave, left me completely flabbergasted! The reason given for that decision: only bereavement of mother, father, sister or brother could warrant permission of compassionate leave. 'Ridiculous', I thought, and felt terribly upset.

Two months later, Sgt Whipps informed me that if I paid my passage at a special rate I could have two weeks UK leave.

I returned to the UK on a charter flight, and after all the flying by service aircraft, that felt like pure luxury! It only took a half of the time to return home, and when my Dad met me at RAF Hendon, I couldn't believe that I had returned to England so quickly. It was 0200 by the time my flight touched down and as I walked into the waiting-room, Tommy had already arrived to meet me.

"Hello Peter, welcome home," my Dad said, hugging me.

"Hi there Dad, it's good to see you!" I answered.

"Your Mum's at home," Tommy said, "making you some bacon and eggs, that's assuming you still like them!"

"Yes, great," I said, my mouth watering at the very thought of it.

"I see you've bought a new car, Dad," I observed, as we approached the vehicle.

"Yes Son, poor old Cuvvie was clapped out," Dad remarked, "So I bought this Humber Hawk."

"It looks good," I said.

"It is extremely reliable," Dad explained, "Mind you, I have only had it a short while."

As I humped my kitbag up the stairs to the flat, my nose began to twitch, 'Hmm...' I thought, 'bacon and eggs frying'.

By the time Tommy inserted his key into the front door lock, it was 0330 hrs. Lucky had already started to bark his head off, and Mum shouted at him to be quiet.

"Peter, darling," my Mum grabbed hold of me, "It's wonderful to see you."

"Hello, Mum," I answered, hugging her.

After my meal I went to bed and slept until 1500 hrs the next day. We had a lot to talk about, so Mum, Dad, Christine and I sat around for hours, just chatting about everything that had happened since we had last met.

"I'll spend a couple of days at home," I told Mum and Dad, "Then I'll go to see Auntie for a week, and then return home for the rest of my leave."

"That's all right with us dear," Mum answered.

I arrived at Piccadilly Station, Manchester, but of course, Uncle Walt did not come to meet me. I felt particularly sad, knowing that I would never see him again. I reached the house, knocked on the old oak-panelled door, and my Auntie opened it.

"Ee – I am right glad to see you dear," she said, with the tears streaming down her old, wrinkled face.

"Me too, Auntie," I answered.

Auntie and I spent a lot of time visiting, shopping together, and calling on Ruth and Ronnie. One evening I said, "I would like to go dancing, Auntie."

"Why don't you go to the Co-op Hall at Bacup," she replied, "There's a dance there twice a week."

On the Wednesday evening I went to the Co-op and, as I sat there rolling a cigarette, a girl came up to me and asked me to dance. After we had danced a quickstep Sarah said, "Let's sit the next one out."

"All right," I agreed, so we sat down, while I proceeded to roll a cigarette.

"Can I roll one for you?" Sarah asked.

"Are you sure you are able to roll a cigarette?" I asked.

"Of course I can!" she answered indignantly, "I roll them for my Dad."

As she sat on my lap, rolling a cigarette for me, Sarah asked, "Can I roll one for myself, Peter?"

"Of course you can," I replied.

Sarah made a particularly good job of it, and the two of us sat there, just relaxing.

The week at Auntie's passed all too quickly. I had been out with Sarah every evening and felt sad at having to say goodbye to her. I felt even more sorry at having to say goodbye to Auntie, but I had to see something of my Mum and Dad before returning to the Middle East.

During the last few days of my leave I spent quite a lot of time with Dad at the television studios at Lime Grove, Shepherds Bush. Tommy still played with the Eric Robinson Orchestra and for the *Black and White Minstrel Show* in the West End of London. I enjoyed mixing with the musicians and met up with many of my old friends again: George Chisholm, Andy McDevitt and, of course, Kenny Baker. They were pleased to hear that I still played music professionally, even though in a Military Band. Eric Robinson told me to contact him after I had finished my time in the RAF. It seemed as if my musical future might be assured after all.

Rachel and Tommy took me to RAF Hendon in the Humber and at 0730 I took off back to Cyprus. It had made a pleasant break to go home on leave, but I felt glad to get back to playing once more.

The next trip for the band turned out to be a flying visit to RAF Luqa in Malta. What a nightmare journey for us all! I had never really felt completely at ease in the air, although the band had flown thousands of miles during its tour of the Middle East. We were about halfway to our destination when suddenly one of the port engines of the four-engined Hastings spluttered, then ceased to function. The co-pilot walked up and down the plane reassuring everyone.

"We can, if need be, fly on just two engines," he said. "Although only one of the engines has packed up, it is possible that the other port engine might seize up also, but we can manage the rest of the journey on two starboard engines, so don't worry!" The remainder of the journey felt a bit scary, but the band arrived safely at Malta, albeit using three engines.

RAF Luqa didn't have much to offer as camps go, but as No.6 Regional Band would only be there for two weeks, it didn't really matter. The camp, as they generally are, was situated quite a distance from the town – in this case Valetta, the Maltese capital – and had a virtually non-existent bus service. Inevitably, if we wished to go anywhere other than duty calls, we musicians had to use taxis.

The mornings were taken up either by rehearsals in the Band Room or on the Square for the 'Beating of the Retreat'. On the second day, after the morning rehearsal, Bob booked a taxi and then he, Barry, Brian and I went into Valetta for a look around. There appeared to be two main pastimes for the people of Malta – brass bands and housey-housey (lotto or bingo). Everywhere we walked in the town we could hear either a brass band or a game of housey-housey being played.

My companions and I sat down outside a restaurant, ordered a beer each and listened to the brass band, which turned out to be an exceptionally skilful one and we were really impressed. We must have been sitting there for more than an hour when suddenly there came a succession of loud bangs from the harbour.

"That's gunfire," I said.

"It certainly is," Barry answered, "I wonder what that's all about?"

"Let's go and see," Bob shouted.

With that, we gulped down our beer and rushed down the street to the seafront. An American gunboat had encountered some difficulties two miles out at sea and seemed to be sinking fast. The gunfire had been a distress single. As we stood there, leaning against the handrails, we were astounded to see so many boats and ships rushing out to the aid of the vessel in distress. Miraculously, nobody had been seriously hurt, but the boat did sink and, strangely, we never did find out exactly what had happened.

"Let's go down to The Gut," Bob suggested.

"The Gut?" Brian said, quizzically. "What on earth is that?"

"The Gut," Bob answered, "is world famous for its bars and brothels."

"We had a taste of that in Baghdad," I said reluctantly, "And look what happened there!"

"The street itself and some of the bars are not out of bounds," Bob went on, "and we can't leave Malta without at least seeing it, can we now?"

So finally, after a little arguing, we lads walked down the famous 'Gut'. There were literally hundreds of bars, some marked with a sign 'Out of Bounds to all Military Personnel'. After walking for a while, we finally selected 'The Hangman's Cove' to have a drink. It was a dark, dingy-looking place, but that must have been the intention.

As we had plenty of time to enjoy our drinks and see some more of the sights of Malta, we relaxed and took it easy. We boarded a bus for Selima, a small fishing town not far from Valetta. After arriving at our destination, we strolled up and down the streets.

"There isn't a lot to see here," Brian remarked, to which the rest of us agreed, so after a couple of drinks we returned back to the RAF Camp.

The following day we were kept extremely busy. At 0730, we had the 'Beat the Retreat' rehearsal, followed by another rehearsal, this time for the evening concert, the latter to be held in the Camp Theatre. The marching practise went satisfactorily, so at 10.00 Sergeant Whipps called the band into the Rehearsal Room. Another novelty number had been added to the programme. I changed instruments from the Eb clarinet (high reed) to the Bb clarinet in order to play Mozart's Clarinet Concerto. Instead of just playing the piece of music sitting down, in the usual manner, I would be walking up and down the aisles among the audience while playing. Having memorised it, I could concentrate more on showmanship. That same afternoon, while we musicians were relaxing on our beds, Harry Whipps appeared with the results of the Promotion Exams. Sergeant Whipps had been promoted to Flight Sergeant, Corporal Pullen to Sergeant, and there were to be two new corporals in the band, Barry, and Pete Ramsden. As for me, I now had the title of Senior Aircraftman (SAC), which did not mean overmuch (although the extra money would come in handy!).

As usual, the concert was successful and after the 'Beating of the Retreat' ceremony, an Officers' Mess function, plus a couple of parades, No.6 Regional Band was on its way again, back to RAF Episkopi.

By September 1956 the troubles in Cyprus were dying down a little, so the musicians were able to go out more often. I had a gig at RAF Akrotiri near Limassol. Five other musicians and I hired a cab, then proceeded to the camp. 'The New Hatters' were going to prove to be a popular group: Me on alto sax/clarinet/MC/vocals, Albert on trumpet, Bob on trombone, Tony on string bass, Dave on drums and Fred on piano/keyboards.

As we approached the NAAFI, Tony noticed two men behind one of the huts, acting rather suspiciously.

"We had better not tackle them," I said, "They may be armed."

As we got out of the taxi, we saw two armed guards, along with an SP Sergeant.

"There are two men acting suspiciously behind one of the huts over there," I told them.

With that, the guards rushed to where I had pointed. After a scuffle, a couple of shots rang out. The two men were, in fact, EOKA terrorists, planting an explosive device under one of the huts. One of them had pulled out a revolver when challenged, but the Sergeant had fired first, twice. After thanking my friends and I for our prompt action, the Sergeant, along with the two guards, escorted the terrorists to the Guard Room.

"Phew, that was a close call!" Bob exclaimed, wiping his forehead, "I hope there aren't any more of those blighters about."

The security guards searched the camp thoroughly, but the terrorists were obviously alone and did not have the opportunity to plant any more explosives. Everyone enjoyed the dance and the 'New Hatters' were invited back to play at RAF Akrotiri at a later date.

One day, as I walked through the band compound, I stopped for a moment to light a cigarette and as I stood looking out to sea, wondering about everybody at home, I heard voices whispering and laughing. The sounds were coming from our tent. The lads inside had zipped the tent shut and there were obviously quite a few of them in there. What I heard made me extremely angry. I recognised Barry's voice immediately, and the things he said confirmed my suspicions.

"Ee, that twerp looked like a drowned rat," Barry whispered.

"Yes, it must have taken him a week, to dry out," Bob laughed.

"It served him jolly well right," that sounded like Brian's voice. They were all laughing. I now knew what I had suspected all along, but had not wished to believe, that my friend had been the instigator of the ducking in the bath!

'Hmph…' I muttered to myself, 'That's supposed to be my friend'.

I didn't say anything to Barry, but from then on I tried to avoid him as much as possible, which turned out to be difficult, as we shared the same tent…

Aden would be the next destination of No.6 Regional Band MEAF and the final tour before we were transferred to RAF Eastleigh, Kenya, for the remainder of our service abroad. We packed up our instruments, ceremonial uniforms and personal belongings, then proceeded as usual to load up the aeroplane. We would be flying in a RAF Valetta on this occasion and the journey shouldn't take too long.

We arrived at RAF Khormaksar in Aden at midday and the heat must have been the most intense we had experienced in all the time spent abroad – a humid heat, not dry as in Egypt, nor with sea breezes like Cyprus. We certainly could not stay in it for too long, even when swimming. Most of us were soon afflicted with heat rashes, which was amazing when you consider that the band had been abroad for nearly two years. The River Euphrates became our favourite place for swimming and we spent many happy hours there.

One evening out in Aden stood out in my mind for years to come. The band had been playing in the Officers' Mess at RAF Khormaksar, finishing at 2130 hours. After we had changed into our civilian clothes, Brian suggested going into the town for a drink. As usual, this idea was met with approval by everyone, and after hiring taxis, off we went. We wandered from bar to bar until we decided that we had enough, and went back to the taxi rank. Bob, Brian and myself went in one taxi and the remainder in another.

On the way back to camp, the cab driver asked if he could stop for a few moments at his house, to pick up something. We didn't care, besides we were quite merry, after having consumed quite a few beers. The taxi went off the main road and stopped outside a small brick house, which stood among a few mud huts. By this time it was 0230 and the lads were half asleep.

The taxi driver got out, saying, "I won't be a minute Effendis," and dashed into his little brick house.

Suddenly the car became surrounded by Arabs, who started by shaking it, and waving their fists at us inside.

'Oh no', I thought. 'We've really had it this time!'

The doors of the vehicle were pulled open, we were dragged out of the taxi and viciously kicked and punched. The wail of a police siren turned out to be our salvation, followed by the rumble of army vehicles as the Special Police and Commandos appeared on the scene. They arrested the Arabs, but we also were arrested. We were allowed to go free to our billet that night, but would have to appear before Waggie the following day.

Flying Officer Wagner did not seem at all pleased. After my two fellow culprits and I had been frog-marched into his office, he glared at us and asked,

"What have you three got to say for yourselves?"

I explained what had happened.

"It doesn't sound a particularly likely story to me," the officer snapped, and turned his attention to the other two.

They confirmed my story and Waggie summed up by saying that he would accept our explanation, but we would still have to appear, before the Camp CO...

Squadron Leader Johnson looked up from his desk and stared at the three musicians facing him.

"Flying Officer Wagner has given your account to me and the reasons given for being out of bounds," the Camp CO addressed us sternly, then continued, "The taxi driver has confirmed your story, but unfortunately Queen's Regulations state that any military personnel caught out of bounds *for any reason whatsoever* shall be punished. Therefore, I would normally be compelled to sentence you to fatigues and confinement to barracks, but firstly you are members of a touring band responsible for entertaining the troops, secondly, you are needed for parades and third, you are flying back to Cyprus tomorrow. Therefore I will leave the disciplinary punishment up to F/O Wagner, now *dismiss!*"

I couldn't quite make up my mind whether that was good news or bad. 'Anyway', I thought, 'We shouldn't be punished at all, as it wasn't our fault that the taxi driver took us to his village'.

The next few weeks proved extremely hectic, as we had to prepare for the move to RAF Eastleigh, near Nairobi, Kenya, where No.6 Regional Band was going to spend the last few months of its Middle Eastern Tour. Before that, we had concerts, parades and officers' mess functions to play for, and as most of the musicians were looking forward to the move, time began to drag, even though we were exceptionally busy. As we had so many commitments, F/O Wagner had postponed his decision whether to punish us offenders until the band had settled down in Kenya.

The final 'Beating of the Retreat' ceremony in Cyprus, took place in Nicosia itself, and the band had a couple of new movements to add to our routine. We formed up in the usual manner, then began to march, with Drum Major Whipps at the head of the columns. After going through the usual routine of counter marching, changing from quick to slow march, and the Drum Major performing with his mace, the two new movements were introduced.

"Band... marching on the spot, *begin*," Harry Whipps ordered. Next, two double taps on the side drum, and the Drum Major raised the mace, high into the air in front of him. As he brought down the mace, the musicians from the centre column took three paces to the left, forming two columns instead of three. Next, after two three-beat drum rolls, the band marched off once more. At a signal from the mace, held vertically and stretched out to the right, the right-hand column did a 'u-turn' to the right and the left-hand column to the left, thus forming a circle. After the circle had been completed, the Drum Major, who stood at the centre, raised his mace. Double taps and a three-beat drum roll signalled the band to look up. The instruments were then lowered and as the mace was brought down, the band came to a halt.

March cards were changed next, and some light music played: 'Puppet on a String' and 'La Paloma Blanca' into the march 'High School Cadets'. As the musicians were playing the latter, the warning came from the drums, Harry Whipps raised his mace and the band commenced 'marching on the spot'. Half the circle moved to the right and the other half to the left. Harry marched through the circle and the band formed a straight line behind him, then carried on marching in that formation. Next, the line broke at the centre, half to the left, half to the right, making a 'u'-turn to come up behind the Drum Major, forming two columns. Finally, after breaking up into the original three columns, the band played the (by now familiar) Nimrod, Sunset and Last Post, followed by the Padre's speech and Reveille.

At last the preparations for the move to RAF Eastleigh had been finalised and, in November 1956, No.6 Regional Band transferred to Kenya. There were going to be more exciting times before we returned finally to England.

RAF Eastleigh wasn't, by any means, the best camp we had been to, but at least the trouble with the Mau-Mau terrorists had almost died out, so we musicians were able to move about more freely than before. As usual, the billets were in a remote part of the camp, but this time, instead of sand, we had to contend with long grass, inhabited by poisonous creatures.

When we had settled in, Waggie called for the other two offenders and me to come before him to answer for the 'Out of Bounds' charge.

"Unfortunately..." he began, "Even though your story had been corroborated by the taxi driver, I have been instructed by the Camp CO at Khormaksar to administer a minor punishment. Therefore, starting tomorrow, the three of you will be confined to camp for one week, and be given seven days Jankers (extra duties)."

I had to report to the Guardroom every morning and evening to clean out the cells, also to perform other light duties. Although the punishment did not seem that severe, I begrudged doing it on principle. But it only lasted seven days, and that quickly passed.

During the second week at RAF Eastleigh, I boarded the bus for Nairobi, intending to have a look around. The bus arrived at the terminus and the passengers were unloaded. I felt quite surprised to see how modern everything appeared to be. The bus terminal itself looked rather like Victoria Coach Station in London. There were inspectors on duty and timetables attached to the bus shelters. *Askaris* (Kenya Police officers) were everywhere and I wondered why there were so many of them. I had only taken a few steps when two askaris confronted me.

"Have you any means of identification?" the taller of the two demanded. I reached into my inside jacket pocket and immediately, the policeman pointed his rifle at me.

"Very slowly, if you please," he warned.

I pulled out my 1250 and gave it to him. After carefully scrutinising it the policeman handed the identification card back to me, thanking me politely. Finally the two of them went off to check on the other passengers.

There were plenty of shops to look at in Nairobi and I felt pleasantly surprised to see Woolworth's and Boot's stores. After browsing around for a while, I walked down a side street and observed that there were 'Out of Bounds' signs on some of the bars. By the time I walked into the Roxy Club on Union Street it was 1830hrs. A three piece band was playing – alto sax, violin and drums. They were not all that proficient, but it was better than no entertainment at all.

I had been sitting by myself for about thirty minutes, chatting to the African bartender, when I saw three Europeans sitting at a table in a far corner of the club.

'They look like mother, father, and daughter', I thought. 'I wonder if they are English?'

"What do you think, Osundu?"

"Probably English, Bwhana, why don't you ask them?"

"*Santasana* Osundu, I think I'll do just that," I replied (I had already learned one or two words of Swahili).

With that, I picked up my glass and walked over to the trio.

"Good evening, excuse me for intruding, but I couldn't help but wonder whether or not you are English?"

Robert Garth-Jones answered me first. "We certainly are, and please don't apologise. In fact, we were wondering the same thing about you."

Robert introduced me to his wife Janine and daughter Jennifer.

'Here I go again', I thought. '*Another* beautiful girl, this time in Kenya'.

The Garth-Jones family had lived on their farm, just on the outskirts of Nairobi, for eight years. Robert had been an engineer in England but when given an opportunity to buy the farm in Kenya, had leapt at the chance. Unfortunately, the Mau-Mau terrorist uprising had affected their living to a certain extent, but now that things were quietening down, the farm had begun to flourish once more. Robert's wife Janine, besides helping on the farm, worked as a part-time interpreter at Eastleigh Airport. Besides speaking Swahili, she also had fluent German, French, Spanish and Italian. Their daughter Jennifer looked like a model: beautiful, blonde and a little older than myself, having just reached her twenty-first birthday. I felt very physically attracted to her.

After spending a few pleasant hours chatting, Robert gave me a lift back to RAF Eastleigh and Janine invited me to spend the following weekend with them at the farm.

The routine continued much the same as before, rehearsals in the Band Room, marching practise, concerts... I had received a letter from my dear Auntie, telling me that she still missed me a lot, also to say that Ruth had given birth to another son – David. I wrote back to her, saying that I would be coming to see her soon. There were only another three months to go before the band completed its tour abroad.

We had been engaged to perform at a charity concert in the Opera House, Nairobi, so the following two days were spent rehearsing for that event. Sergeant Pullen summoned the musicians to the Band Room and the librarian passed the music around for the programme. Ever since Harry Whipps had introduced the idea of 'novelty numbers', the programmes had become much more interesting. Next to be highlighted were the tubas, playing 'The Hippopotamus Song' (Mud, mud, glorious mud!) By this time, as their term of service had come to an end, some of the musicians were due for 'demob'' and four of them were replaced – two cornets, a tuba and a side drummer, which unfortunately meant more marching practise than usual, to enable the newcomers to fit in.

I invited Robert, Janine and Jennifer Garth-Jones to the concert. At 1900 hours the band boarded the coach for the Opera House. On arrival, I found the Garth-Joneses already there to greet me. Jennifer appeared to be quite excited.

"I've never been to a military band concert," she said.

"You will enjoy it, I'm sure," I assured her.

The No.6 Regional Band opened their performance with our signature tune, 'The Royal Air Force March'. The hall was filled to capacity and the applause almost raised the roof. 'Waggie' saluted the audience and turned to the band, tapping the music stand with his baton, then raised his arms in preparation for the next piece. The tuba player stood up to perform his novelty solo. The audience laughed at the humorous parts of the piece and clapped at the technical brilliance of the soloist in the more serious parts. The rest of the performance went very well and was warmly appreciated by one and all.

I packed my weekend case, ready for my visit to Robert Garth-Jones' farm. I had been given a weekend pass and Robert collected me outside of the camp gates. When we arrived at the farm, Janine and Jennifer were there to greet us. The dairy farm was colossal, stretching over three thousand acres. In my childhood days I had spent some time on a farm in Lancashire, but there could be no comparison between the latter and 'Rhino's Reach' (Why the place had been named that, not even Robert knew!) Jennifer led the way to my room. We climbed up a unique staircase covered by tiger skin. Finally, after two hundred steps, she opened the door of the bedroom. It looked quite cosy, and through the window I could see Mount Kilimanjaro in the distance. That of course was no new experience to me, as I could see the mountain each morning, at closer quarters.

The following morning Janine awakened me with a cup of tea.

"I'm sorry to disturb you so early," she apologised, "But I suspect that it is not really early for you!"

I gratefully accepted the tea and confirmed that 6am was not too early. After breakfast I went for a stroll with Jennifer and she took me on a tour of the farm. There were the usual things one would expect to find on a dairy farm, but in addition to those, there were a few animals that are peculiar to Africa. For instance, Jennifer had a pet lion, with only one tooth, called 'Fang'. Robert had found him as a cub, caught in a trap, almost dead. Janine and Jennifer had bottle fed him, but although he became quite affectionate, he had a nervous disposition. The lion nestled up to me, sensing that I had a fondness for animals.

"Just tickle him behind the ears," Jenny said. "He loves that."

I did as suggested and the tiger laughed, exposing his single tooth, then rolled over and over in the long grass.

"Now he wants to play," Jenny explained, "Just like a little child."

Jenny and I played with 'Fang' for a short while, then Jambo and Santa, the twin chimpanzees, joined in.

"Phew!" I puffed, "They certainly do wear you out, don't they Jenny?"

"That's an understatement!" she replied, laughing.

After lunch we were sitting out on the veranda when Robert made a suggestion.

"How about a drive down to Mombasa tomorrow, Peter?"

"That sounds fine to me," I answered.

"That's tomorrow sorted out then," Robert continued, "But what shall we do today?"

"I know," Jenny suggested, "Let's have a musical evening. Have you brought your clarinet, Peter?"

"Yes I have," I replied.

"Mummy plays the piano, Daddy strums the guitar, I sing a little, and Jambo and Santa bang the drums," Jenny said.

After dinner we all gathered around Janine, who was seated at the piano. Robert had a Spanish guitar and the twin chimpanzees sat together on the drum stool. What an amazing sight and an even more amazing sound! With Fang thumping his tail against the bass drum, and cymbals, the noise was tremendous, but strangely enough exceptionally rhythmic. I thoroughly enjoyed the evening and with the strains of 'When the Saints Come Marching In' echoing throughout the farm, and I'm sure far into the surrounding landscape, everyone seemed to have been entertained.

On Sunday morning everyone got up early and prepared for the journey to Mombasa. Janine made a picnic lunch and together with 'Fang' and the twins in the back of the estate wagon, we were soon on our way. The beaches were beautiful, with a clear blue sky and the waves lapping over golden sands; the perfect setting for swimming and sunbathing. The animals were just as excited as the humans, and seeing the water, the three pets jumped up and down, rocking the car and screeching with delight.

"We'll have to find a deserted spot, so that the animals can go into the water too," Jenny said.

"I know just the place," Robert answered, and drove quite a way before eventually stopping. "All out, here we are!" he said.

Robert parked the car, and everyone, including the animals clambered out. I held Jambo and Santa in my arms and Jenny held onto Fang's leash. We scrambled down the bank and onto the secluded beach. I started to realise that animals were much more fun that people – more reliable and trustworthy. Fang, Jambo and Santa chased one another in and out of the water while the rest of us lay sunbathing on the beach. I sat watching the chimps for a while, Jambo making sand pies with a bucket and Santa knocking them down again.

'They really are like children', I thought.

The climax to the day had to be the picnic. Everyone knows that chimpanzees are intelligent and quite amusing, but Jambo and Santa were the funniest pair of animals I had ever seen.

Janine passed the sandwiches and cakes around. Jambo held a sandwich up to his nose, sniffed at it, then opened it up, closed it again and handed it back again.

"What's wrong with it you, silly boy?" she asked. "It's your favourite, banana."

Santa held out her sandwich to her brother, which he took and munched without hesitation.

"Well, would you believe that?" Janine said with utter amazement, "It was identical to the other one, but because it was Santa's, he has eaten it!"

After an exhilarating swim, my friends and I returned to 'Rhino's Reach'. That evening I had to return to camp, but as I had really enjoyed my weekend, I didn't mind too much.

While in Kenya, I had found another friend, Gerry, the Chief Game Warden at the National Game Park in Nairobi. We met one evening while I was having a drink with Jenny at the Roxy Club. Gerry looked more like an Australian than an Englishman, with his bush hat, khaki drill shirt and shorts and heavy suntan. He was a very charismatic person and both Jenny and I took to him immediately.

"Would you like to come with me on my inspection round of the Park, one day?" Gerry asked.

Both Jenny and I accepted the offer.

"I'm not quite sure of our work schedule, Gerry," I said, "But I will let you know."

The first 'Beating of the Retreat' in Kenya, would be held at RAF Eastleigh, so the usual preparations were made and rehearsals began. The band lined up in their usual formation: three ranks of nine musicians in each, with the Drum Major facing them.

"In addition to the routine marches, we will be playing one or two new ones," F/S Whipps informed us.

The Librarian passed the march cards around to each musician. As well as the RAF 'Top Brass', a few high ranking USAF Officers were going to attend, so 'The Star Spangled Banner' was a must!

"Band!" the Drum Major ordered, "Band, atten...tion, Band ready!" Harry continued, "Into line in three columns of route, righ...t turn!" He then marched smartly to the front of the band with the Bandmaster to the rear,

"From now on, the signals will be taken from the drums and the mace," the Drum Major concluded.

With that, after two double taps and one three-beat drum roll, the mace, which had been held high, came down, then the band marched off to the 'RAF March' A new variation had been added, the band forming a 'v' instead of a circle. After the 'counter-march', while marching in quick time, the musicians, at the signal from drums and mace, filtered into two columns behind the Drum Major, to form the 'v'.

The Band came to a halt, the two columns facing inwards, then the Bandmaster conducted the 'sing-along'. Well-known tunes were played, e.g. 'Little Brown Jug', 'Lovely Bunch of Coconuts' and many others. After the usual Finale, the band marched off.

Gerry picked me up, then Jennifer, in his land rover, ready for our tour of the 'National Game Park'. As we drove along chatting, a male rhinoceros chased after us for a while, but gave up the chase when he caught sight of a female. Then we had a race with some antelope, which we lost. It really did have the makings of an exciting day. At lunchtime we stopped for a picnic in the shade of a tree and relaxed for a while.

"Whereabouts in England are you from, Gerry?" I asked.

"Morden in Surrey," came the sleepy reply.

"I don't believe it!" I said, with surprise, "That's where my grandparents' house is."

"That surely is a coincidence," Gerry said, raising one eyebrow.

The three of us sat talking for a while, then climbed into the Land Rover for the remainder of Gerry's inspection of the park. After travelling for a while, Gerry slowed down to let a family of chimpanzees cross the dusty road. As the vehicle came to a halt, three of the animals jumped onto the vehicle's bonnet and pulled funny faces at us through the windscreen. I replied by doing the same thing. To my horror, the chimps urinated over the windscreen, then quickly scurried away. Jenny and Gerry laughed , but I didn't find the event quite so amusing, as I had borne the brunt of the 'shower' By this time the evening began to draw in.

"I think we had better return to town before nightfall," Gerry said, but he had barely finished speaking when a loud screech made us jump!

"Sounds as if those poachers are at it again," he exclaimed, jumping from the vehicle and rushing towards a clump of trees.

Jenny and I followed closely behind but the sight that met our gaze filled us with horror: A gazelle had its leg caught in a very nasty-looking trap and in trying to struggle free it had only made things worse.

"I will have to put the poor thing out of its misery," Gerry said, apologetically. With one shot from his rifle, the animal would suffer no more.

"Can't anything be done to stop those barbarians?" I asked.

"We do all we can," Gerry answered, "But it is obviously not enough."

We climbed into the Land Rover once more, preparing to return to Nairobi. By this time, darkness had fallen and as we were approaching the exit from the Game Park, the headlights lit up the bush, just in time for us to see a lion pounce on a gazelle. It all happened so quickly but according to Gerry it was a rare sight, even though he inspected the park every day. We returned to Gerry's home for a drink, to listen to records and have a chat.

"We must do this again sometime," Gerry offered.

Both Jenny and I agreed. The evening passed pleasantly, then Gerry drove Jenny and me home.

Once a month the Military Band performed at the Officers Mess dinner; usually there was nothing out of the ordinary about these functions, but on this occasion, something very extraordinary occurred after 'tunes and toasts' (when the Regimental March of each branch of the Armed Forces present is played and glasses are raised to Her Majesty the Queen and any dignitaries present). After the meal, while the band played light music, the officers, their wives and guests chatted and took drinks, but then, much to everyone's surprise, the commanding officer and the camp padre began to play leapfrog! Many of the officers followed suit, and before long, the room was in an uproar. Waggie was horrified, and although the rest of the lads in the band were laughing, it wasn't really funny, just childishly ridiculous. Without further ado, Waggie dismissed the band, and we retreated to the coach that was been waiting outside for us. As F/L Wagner climbed into the vehicle, the Camp Adjutant (2nd in command) shouted at him.

"Who told you to leave, Bandmaster?"

"With all due respect, Sir," Waggie answered, standing at attention, "There are many valuable musical instruments here, which incidentally, are the property of Her Majesty the Queen, and as I have been unable to attract the attention of the CO to ask permission to leave, I decided to use my discretion, and quietly retreat."

I was impressed by the Bandmaster's clever answer. Besides being quite diplomatic, the mention of Her Majesty's property put paid to any further questions and the Band returned to their quarters without argument.

The remaining three weeks at RAF Eastleigh were really busy ones for our band and we did not have many leisure moments. I did not have the opportunity to see Jenny very often, but when I did, I made the most of it! One evening Jenny met me outside of the camp gates, accompanied by Gerry. As I approached, I noticed that the pair of them appeared to be embarrassed.

"Hello you two, anything wrong?" I enquired.

"No, of course not," Jenny answered, but I sensed that something was amiss.

"Where shall we go this evening?" I broke the silence.

"Let's go back to my place for a drink and listen to records," Gerry suggested.

Although I liked Gerry, I would have preferred to spend the evening alone with Jenny, but during the course of the evening Jenny remained sulky and rather quiet and every time I looked at her she turned her head away. Although I had treated the relationship as casual, I had become particularly fond of her.

"Can we have a word in private, Jenny?" I asked her.

"What about?" she snapped.

I turned to Gerry, "Would you mind giving me a lift back to camp, please Gerry? I think I'll have an early night."

As we drove along, I tried to make conversation with Jenny, but she had become withdrawn, which was most unusual for her. I bade Gerry and Jenny goodnight and said finally, "It has been lovely knowing you, Jenny. I don't know what's happened between us, but take good care of yourself, won't you?" She didn't answer me, but as Gerry drove off, I could see that she had tears in her eyes.

I never did see Jenny again, but a few days later as I sat drinking in the Roxy, Gerry came up to me.

"Hallo, me old mate, how are you?" he said.

"Not bad," I answered, "But what the hell was going on the other night with you and Jenny?"

He looked embarrassed.

"I'm sorry if you've been hurt, Peter, but... well, Jenny and I have fallen in love with each other and she just didn't know how to tell you."

I explained that Jenny and I had become friends but no more, so I couldn't understand why she had behaved like that towards me.

The Middle Eastern tour of No.6 Regional Band had reached its conclusion and we musicians were busy packing up our belongings, ready for the long journey back to England. It had been educational, exciting, sometimes boring, and quite often dangerous, but all of us were excited at the thought of returning home to our families. It was March 1957, we lads had spent two and a half years abroad, some without a break. I had, at least, been home on leave. It would seem strange not to wake up to see either the desert sands from the tent or Mount Kilimanjaro out of the window of the billet. Instead I would be going home to see houses and buses passing from the window of the flat.

The return flight to England was uneventful and so another era in my life had passed!

The Author, in Egypt, 1954.

Andreanna Kyriakou, Cyprus 1954.

Serial No. 38/58

R.A.F. Form 856

ROYAL AIR FORCE

Certificate of Service

of

Official No. 4128164

Rank Senior Aircraftman.

Surname BRADBURY.

First names Peter Grayson

Date of birth 10th October 1935

Civil occupation Musical Assistant

Date of last enlistment 5th May 1953

Trade in R.A.F. on enlistment Assistant Musician

Date of Transfer to Reserve (Class ....)

Date of Discharge 4th May 1958

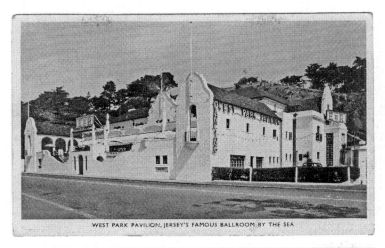

WEST PARK PAVILION, JERSEY'S FAMOUS BALLROOM BY THE SEA

Rashid Street, Baghdad.

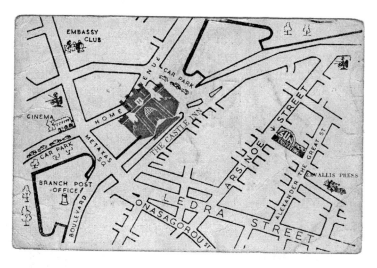

Nicosia town centre.

Author in blue ceremonial uniform, Episkopi, Cyprus, 1955.

Author and Barry Swales in white ceremonial uniform,
Cyprus 1955.

Author with WRAF girls, Episkopi, 1955.

MEAF Band, Baghdad, 1955.

MEAF Band Egypt, 1955.

In 1955, 'Professor' Jimmy Edwards (comedian), Janet Brown (of *Busy American Working Girl* fame) and Harry 'Piano' Jacobson flew out to the Middle East to join our band in Cyprus for a three-week tour.

I had met Jimmy and Janet previously on Hughie Green's *Opportunity Knocks* show. Jimmy had a particularly dry sense of humour. My favourite of his sketches were the 'School Classroom' ones, in which 'Professor' Jim would stand before the class, waving a thin cane back and forth.

Suddenly there is a noise from one of the schoolboys and Jimmy erupts, handlebar moustache twitching vigorously.

"Hey you... boy at the back there, fidgeting noisily, what's your name?"

"Shufflebottom, Sir!" the boy answers nervously.

In another sketch, Professor Jim would be sitting at the head of the class and on dipping his quill pen into his inkwell and touching the pen-tip with his tongue, would say:

"They don't make Scotch like they used to!"

Another memorable classroom gag of Jim's was:

"Hey there, boy in the third row, next to the ugly one with the yellow buck teeth. Put out that cigarette. If Mother Nature had intended you to smoke, she would have provided you with a chimney... Ha-ha-ha, she has!"

The song 'Busy American Working Girl' (from the show by the same title) was sung at high speed and could only be delivered by someone with Janet's remarkable ability with that type of song.

Their joint comedy sketches caused uproar with service audiences, being a bit 'near the knuckle' though not overmuch. Janet was a brilliant comedienne in her own right, and used to have us 'laughing our socks off'.

Harry 'Piano' Jacobson used to join in with some of the more hilarious sketches, but was more notable for his 'I Love a Piano' song:

> *I love a piano, I love a piano*
> *I love to hear that keyboard play...*

He could be extremely funny too, and I often wondered why he didn't appear in 'drag'.

6. The Return

It seemed strange to be in England again and I felt as if I had returned from another world. No more sand, tents or camels. Never again would I have to struggle against the *khamsin* to keep the tent intact, and above all, sand-free food! The one thing I would miss would be the sun. I loved the hot weather, but luckily for me, the weather in England had turned warm by the time I arrived home. The heat wasn't anyway near as intense as the Middle East, of course, but felt just pleasantly warm. We had been given two weeks leave, before going to our respective home postings.

I soon settled down at home and carried on with my musical studies. During my holiday I went to see Auntie again. I spent one week with her, but unfortunately caught a terrible cold, as it was particularly chilly 'up North!' At the end of my two weeks leave, I reported to the Central Band HQ and was interviewed by Wing Commander Simms.

"I am pleased to inform you, Bradbury, that you will be spending the remainder of your service here at Uxbridge," the Director of Music informed me.

I could hardly believe it; my dream had come true.

"Thank you, Sir," I replied.

'Simmsy' went on, "You will be able to live at home, reporting here each morning and, tours excepted, it will be just like a civvy job."

I thanked the officer again, saluted, then marched smartly out of the office.

My first engagement with the Central Band was to be in Northern Ireland, where we were going to play at RAF

Aldergrove, near Belfast, for an important parade to commemorate the Queen's Official Birthday. I packed my kitbag and suitcase, then travelled to Folkestone by train. The rest of the band were there to greet me and we all went aboard the British Rail ferry en-route for Belfast.

The sea crossing turned out to be the most horrendous journey that I had ever experienced. I didn't feel seasick, but felt extremely queasy! After consuming a couple of beers, I felt a little better, so I strolled onto the deck. Daryl and George both had befriended me recently, just after I had joined RAF Central Band. As fellow musicians, I found them both particularly easy to get along with. We talked for a while, then returned to the bar for more drinks. By this time, I felt considerably better, which didn't seem too surprising, as I had consumed a couple of large whiskeys and a few pints of beer.

We were sitting quietly, sipping our drinks, when I started to feel as if someone's eyes were boring into my back. I turned my head to see one of the musicians staring at me. One of the tuba players, who had a reputation as a bit of a tough guy, was giving me the 'evil eye'.

"I should ignore him, if I were you," Daryl warned.

"Why on earth does he keep staring at me?" I asked.

"He's had too much to drink," George Williams answered. "Take Daryl's advice, and just take no notice of him"!

I rose out of my chair to go to the toilet and as I walked past, Big Jock grabbed hold of my arm and said, "Hey you, are you looking for trouble?"

Being very much a pacifist, I shook off the hand that had grabbed me, stared the big man straight in the eyes and although inwardly nervous said, "I have no quarrel with you, but if you wish to fight, I will accommodate you."

Jock stepped back with a look of amazement on his face and said, "Let's have a drink!" I joined him for one, then returned to my friends.

"I don't know what you said to him, mate," Daryl remarked, "But whatever it was, it certainly did the trick!"

"As you said, it had to be just the drink talking," I concluded.

The Ferry docked at Belfast harbour and we musicians were transferred onto ten-tonners en-route for RAF Aldergrove. We arrived at the camp just in time for dinner, so the rest of the band and I changed clothes, then proceeded to the Airmen's Mess. After the meal, which was not too bad (salad, with fruit and custard to follow), we musicians returned to our billet. That evening George, Daryl and I hired a taxi bound for Belfast. After wandering around a few of the bars, we decided to go ballroom dancing at the Plaza. It had its resident dance orchestra, the Royal Show-band, performing there every evening, and was extremely popular. My two friends and I sat down with our beer at a table and listened to the music, a few big-band jazz numbers, and I felt 'in my element'. During the interval I had a chat with Brendan, the Bandleader.

"Why don't you sit in on the Dixieland numbers, Pete?" he suggested.

"I haven't brought my clarinet," I replied sadly.

"Borrow mine, you're welcome I'm sure," Brendan offered.

It developed into a great evening – 'Jazz-me Blues', 'At the Jazz-Band Ball', Dark-Ttown Strutters Ball', 'The Saints' and 'Bill Bailey Won't You Please Come Home' – to name but a few. Later on in the evening I asked a young woman to dance and enjoyed that so much that I asked her again, then a third time. Her name was Anna and she lived near Belfast. I invited her to join my two friends and me at the table. After the dance we walked Anna to her bus-stop, then caught a taxi back to camp.

The next morning, up at 0600, washed, dressed, and suitably warmed up by a hearty breakfast, the Central Band marched onto parade, at 0830. The Duke of Norfolk represented Her Majesty the Queen and would be taking the 'salute' in her absence. The band played the troops on parade with the Royal Air Force March, followed by Souza's 'High School Cadets'. After the parade had been formed into 'flights' (sections), the 'squadron' (whole parade) was brought to 'attention' by the Station Warrant Officer, who continued to give the 'arms drill' orders…

"Par-ade!" his short, sharp commands echoed across the Square, "Par-ade, atten-*tion*, par-ade slope *arms*, par-ade shoulder *arms*.

The procedure had then to be reversed: "Slo-pe *arms*" then "par-ade stand at *ease* – stand easy!" the SWO concluded.

After thirty minutes, the Duke of Norfolk arrived in a helicopter of 'the Queen's Flight' and the official ceremony commenced. The commands were then given by the Adjutant and the General Salute 'present arms' order was issued, then the Union Jack raised. The inspection followed next and while the Duke inspected the Squadron, the Band played the slow march 'Scipio', 'Puppet on a String' and other light music, until the inspection finished. Finally, it was the band's turn to be given the once-over. The Director of Music stamped smartly to attention, saluted, then escorted His Royal Highness through the ranks of the band. The Duke stopped to have a word with one or two of us musicians, but on that occasion passed me by. The Parade came to an end at 1100 hrs and the we returned to our billet, changed out of our ceremonial uniforms into civilian clothes, then packed in readiness for the journey by ferry back to England.

In September 1957 I would experience my first 'White City Tattoo'. Unfortunately that spectacular no longer exists, but at that time it was tremendously popular. The 'Searchlight Tattoo', performed in the evening at the White City Sports Stadium, West London, consisted of bands from all parts of Great Britain, amalgamated to form a 'massed bands' spectacular. On the first evening of the tattoo, I arrived at the stadium early, to join the rest of the Central Band in the car park. I climbed onto the coach and was greeted by a chorus of 'Come on Bradders, you're late!' I laughed and replied, "Considering that I'm an hour early, that's a joke!" They were quite good fun, those lads in the 'Central Band', probably the mere fact of not having to live with them twenty-four hours a day, added to making an easier relationship between us. I changed into my 'ceremonials', then proceeded with a few of the beer drinkers to the bar.

"We had better only have one," Ginger advised us, "Because we will be on parade for about an hour."

The massed bands lined up side by side, forming a colourful pattern across the arena – the Royal Marine Band, with white helmets, navy blue uniform and white belts; the Irish, Scots and Welsh Guards complete with bearskins, scarlet tunics and blue trousers; the Black Watch, dressed in their best kilts and the RAF Central Band in our light blue uniform, blue peaked caps, gold-braid epaulets and white belts.

After marching in quick, then slow time, and counter-marching, the bands came to a halt. Next the finale, incorporating the same tunes as 'The Beating of the Retreat': Nimrod, Sunset, the Last Post, the Padre's prayer, then the Reveille to round off the performance. Wing Commander Simms conducted the massed bands and we were all marched out of the arena.

I arrived home late that night, and went straight to bed. Although we only had to play for one performance per night, for seven days, I felt thoroughly exhausted. As we had the daytime free, I made the most of it, by practising and studying.

One evening I had to baby-sit my sister while Mum and Dad went out, and I played with her and her toys for a couple of hours then helped her to get ready for bed. After reading a couple of stories to her, she soon fell asleep, so I sat in front of the electric fire in the lounge, reading. I had not been feeling my best at all that day, with a slightly sore throat and headache. I looked at the wall-clock, 'Hmmm,' I thought, '12.30, they ought to be home soon'. Suddenly, I started to cough, my breathing became difficult, and I gasped, choked and passed out.

Luckily for me, Mum and Dad came in five minutes later.

Mum started to panic when she saw me sprawled out on the floor but Dad ran to where I lay and checked my breathing, pulse and heartbeat.

"Ring for an ambulance quickly Rae," he ordered. "I'm not sure what's wrong, but he is feverish and his throat is swollen!" I awoke with a nasty taste of blood in my mouth, my breathing laboured and as my eyes focussed I could see that I had landed up in a hospital bed!

Dad stood by the bedside.

"Don't try to talk, lad," he said softly, "Have no fear, you are in the RAF Hospital, Uxbridge. They have just taken out your tonsils. When we arrived home and found you lying there on the floor, your poor Mum thought that you had gone to The Happy Rocking Jazz Club in the Sky! Thank God you are OK."

I replied, somewhat hesitantly, "I…I'm s…orry Dad, but I just coughed, choked, then don't remember another thing."

After a few days in hospital, then one week convalescing at home, I returned to my duties.

The next engagement – would you believe it – was a weekend playing in Jersey.

'This is going to be terrific', I thought, 'I wonder if I will see Regina?'

We were flown to Jersey by British Airways and it seemed to me as if I had hardly stepped aboard the aircraft before I had to step off again. It was a beautiful day, the island hadn't changed a bit, and I really was looking forward eagerly to that weekend.

The first performance was in the park at St Helier and as my white ceremonial uniform had been handed in on my return from the Middle East, I now had to wear my Best Blue uniform, which I found most uncomfortable, especially in the heat of Jersey. The one thing that pleased me more than anything was not having to play that silly little Eb clarinet anymore. I never had really enjoyed the instrument, although playing as a soloist had given me the experience I needed. At the moment my position as a third clarinettist in the 'B' band, was not giving me much satisfaction musically, but just to play with the Central Band gave me a thrill. After a selection of tunes from the shows *Call me Madam* and *Band Wagon* it was the solo cornettist's turn to shine. The piece chosen, 'Carnival in Venice', was popular mostly with Brass Band audiences. After a flawless performance the audience showed their appreciation and the soloist returned to his seat.

During the course of the afternoon, drinks both alcoholic and non-alcoholic were passed around to us musicians. The hospitality shown to the Central Band was overwhelming.

In the evening, the Band marched along the seafront, playing various marches. As the Band counter-marched outside the West Park Pavilion I spotted Regina. She was talking to her Mother and Father. She didn't notice me at first, but when she did catch sight of me, she waved excitedly.

Regina hadn't changed much since I had last seen her, four years ago. She may have put on a little weight, but that was quite becoming. A meal had been laid on for us musicians at the West Park Pavilion, so as there were two hours to spare before the evening concert, after eating, my two friends and I went for a stroll. As we were walking down the steps, I saw Regina. She had been waiting for me, and as I approached her, greeted she me with a big smile.

"It's been a long time, Peter," she said, grabbing hold of me and kissing me.

I introduced Regina to my two companions, then Daryl said, "I'm sure that you two would like to be alone, we'll go on and have a drink then meet you later, Peter."

True, we did have a lot of things to discuss. Regina spoke first.

"I thought you were going to write to me," she said sadly.

"I intended to," I replied, "But so much has happened since I last saw you, and time goes by so quickly."

"That's true," she agreed.

We went to our favourite bar, the 'Moulin de Lec' at Grave de Lec. Although it was quite early in the evening, the bar looked full. I looked at my watch and said, "We haven't got much time, love, so let's hope that they serve us quickly."

The barman seemed quite efficient and before very long we had our drinks – a John Collins for me and a Babycham for Regina. We sat outside on the balcony, talking over old times.

"Gosh," Regina said. "You have been to as lot of exciting places, Peter."

"Yes," I answered her, "And if it hadn't been for the RAF, I don't suppose I would ever have been any further than Blackpool."

Unfortunately, time waits for no man, so the two friends returned to the West Park Pavilion. The dance hall had been converted into a concert hall and there was a long queue waiting to see the Central Band. Regina's Mother and Father were already there, waiting for her.

As usual, the concert was a success. The RAF March, the Star Spangled Banner and High School Cadets were the opening marches. These were followed by the Overture Light Cavalry and a medley of Glen Miller that made me wish I could play with a jazz band. Every time the band played that type of music my thoughts turned towards my main ambition. 'Would it ever be?' I wondered, 'Maybe one day!' The show finished at 2300 and the musicians sat down to supper. Fortunately, we were not flying home that night, as there was as much free beer as we could drink! I went with the le Geyts to a night club, and didn't return back to the hotel until the early hours.

After saying goodbye to Regina for the second time in my life, I was homeward bound once more.

The next few months were quite hectic, the Central Band being in great demand, playing for parades, concerts and officers mess functions. One morning I was summoned to the Director of Music's office.

"Good morning, Peter," Simmsy addressed me, "Stand easy."

I was surprised at the familiar use of my christian name; usually it was 'Bradbury' or just 'Senior Aircraftsman'.

"Morning Sir," I answered respectfully.

"You are going to be demobbed in three months time," the Wing Commander continued. "I trust that you will be signing on again?"

I thought for a moment before answering, then said, "I have spent nearly five years in the Royal Air Force Music

Services, Sir and wishing to further my career in the world of jazz, I must respectfully decline your kind offer."

Simmsy was displeased and did not conceal the fact.

"You will find 'Civvy Street' very hard Peter. I should think twice if I was you."

I remained adamant, but apologised and thanked the DOM for my time spent at Uxbridge.

One of my favourite engagements, and one that nearly landed me a position as second clarinet with the Halle Orchestra, came about just before I became due for 'demob'.

In April 1958 the Halle Orchestra and Central Band were joining together to perform for a charity concert at the Royal Albert Hall. Sir John Barbirolli would be conducting and there were to be many rehearsals. On that particular occasion I met Pat Ryan, the Principal Clarinettist with the Halle. One of the pieces, the New World Symphony, took a lot of rehearsing to achieve the perfection of balance between the orchestra and the Military Band. During one of the many tea breaks I entered into conversation with Pat.

"I have been listening to you Peter," he said, "and I'm very impressed by what I've heard. We will be losing the Second Clarinet shortly, so why don't you apply for an audition."

I didn't know what to say, as I intended to leave the RAF because I wanted to play jazz, and lo and behold, Pat offered me an opportunity to play with the Halle!

"Thank you Pat, thank you very much," I answered.

It turned out to be a most memorable concert and raised thousands of pounds for children's homes. My family came to support me and confirmed that it had musically been one of the most pleasant evenings they had ever experienced.

That put me in a quandary. Having a chance to stay in Central Band, an opening for me in the Halle and George Clouston, Eric Robinson's right-hand man offering me a summer season in Jersey, I didn't know which way to turn.

The thought of returning to Jersey and playing a dance band helped to make up my mind, however, so after due deliberation I decided to opt for Jersey!

Author with the Eric Robinson Agency Band. Leon Mack (leader) and George Clouston (manager), Jersey, 1958.

7. Back to Civvy Street

On 5th May 1958 '4128164 Bradbury, Peter' once again became plain, ordinary Mr Peter Bradbury. Five years in the RAF had taught me how to take care of myself and had given me the musical experience I would need to further my career but now I was on my way to meet the bandleader Leon Mack and the rest of the band at London's Heathrow Airport, ready for the next chapter in my life.

The Band consisted of piano, string bass, drums, two trumpets, two alto saxes, two tenor saxes and a trombone. The season would last from May to October and the venue would be the West Park Pavilion, St Helier. When we arrived at the airport the band grouped together for a photograph, together with George Clouston. We were to expect Eric Robinson to fly to meet us the next day in readiness for the Grand Opening Night.

We had made our own accommodation arrangements. I had found a rooming house just outside of St Helier, within walking distance of the Dance Hall. Mrs Morgan had bought an old house, renovated it, and rented it out into rooms. Being a widow, she found that having people to stay with her helped alleviate loneliness. I certainly felt surprised to find that the room did not have the facility of hot running water, just a jug and a bowl to wash in! Mrs Morgan supplied breakfast, but for my other meals, I would have to make other arrangements. Still, it did seem quite comfortable and she had a pleasant disposition.

The first hurdle came right at the beginning of the band engagement: During my service in the RAF, I had automatic membership of the Musicians Union, therefore did not have to pay dues or possess a Union Card. Unfortunately, once having left the forces I did not have the same status. Neither myself, nor indeed anyone at the Eric Robinson office, had given that a thought when they engaged me for the summer season. As a matter of course, Union Cards were requested to be shown at the start of an engagement, to prohibit non-union people from taking jobs away from members. Luckily for me, the local Union Representative acted swiftly, made a phone call to headquarters in London, and 'signed me up', thus avoiding my having to make an early return to England.

The opening night commenced, with Eric Robinson having his photograph taken with the Band.

"Nervous lads?" he asked.

Although we were all experienced musicians, a first night had to be something special! We all nodded our heads, then climbed onto the stage. Leon Mack took up his position fronting the band and the remainder of us took our seats ready to play. The hall filled up quickly and the dancing began as Leon led the band on alto sax, with me playing 2nd alto. The first few numbers, waltzes, quicksteps and foxtrots, soon had the people dancing. I played 'Stranger on the Shore' on the clarinet, then the band played one or two novelty numbers and the evening went with a 'swing'.

At the end of the evening, I packed away my instruments and casually strolled along the promenade. With the sea gently lapping over the sands, the full moon reflecting on the water and a light breeze making my face tingle, it was a beautiful evening. I reached the lodging house to find Mrs. Morgan still up, even though she had given a front door key to me so I didn't have to disturb her.

"Hello dear," she greeted me, smiling. "How did your first night go?"

I smiled back. "Fine thanks," I said.

"Would you care to join me for a cup of hot chocolate," she asked.

I gratefully accepted her offer.

Although the wage of £45 per week seemed considerable in 1958, we still couldn't manage on that amount, especially as we had to pay board and lodgings and send money home. Pete the pianist and Derek the trumpet player had both worked in Jersey before and had supplemented their income by potato picking. The job paid extremely well, but could be dangerous, especially in causing back-strain, but even so I joined them. Each morning we arose at 5am, breakfasted, spent six hours in the field, then rested or went for a swim, before playing for the tea dancing in the afternoon. The main problem with potato picking, apart from hurting your back, was that it made your hands sore. On that first day after being out in the field I could hardly move my fingers, they were so sore! But after a few days my hands became accustomed to the hard work and the most important thing was that my pay packet looked a lot bulkier!

I had expected to see Regina, but apparently her family had moved to the South of France, so I would not be seeing her again. Sunday turned out to be my only free day, so instead of lying in, I made full use of my spare time by swimming, horse riding and visiting different parts of the island. I had visited Jersey twice before, so by now I felt almost like a resident. I called in at the Merton Hotel to have a drink and went to look at the 'German War Cemetery'. I occasionally visited the betting shop at St Helier, it being one bad habit I had picked up that I could have done well without, not that I had become an excessive gambler, but there were times, due to boredom, that I had a bet when I could ill-afford it. The main problem with betting, as many a gambler will tell you, is that if one has a big win from a small wager, 'the bug' can take hold. Unfortunately, that happened to me. One day I had been swimming, taken a beef-burger and a beer in one of the restaurants at St Helier, then having time to spare before the tea-dance, wandered into the betting-shop. I wandered around, looking at the runners and riders at the various meetings in England, when I saw a horse that I fancied the name of, 'Peter's Pet'. 'Hmm…' I thought, 'That's a coincidence'. I looked further on three other horses: Wee Pedro, Peter the Great and finally Peter and the Wolf. I decided to have a 5d win 'Yankee', which would cost me 11/- (55p). I stayed to listen to the first race, which 'Extel' broadcast over the 'Tannoy'. Peter's Pet won at 20-1, making 21/- running on to the other three horses. I felt a hot flush of excitement running through me, but remembering that I had never been lucky, went back to my lodgings to change ready for the tea-dance. The dance-floor reminded me of the desert, in fact there weren't many people in the hall for the remainder of the afternoon. It really had been one of the hottest days of the year, but as per usual 'the show must go on!' As nobody got up to dance, Mack turned to face the audience.

"I can see that we'll have to wake you lot up!" he joked. "How about a Paul Jones?" The music started up, Mack climbed down from the stage, picked a partner, then walked to the centre of the hall. "Come along Ladies and Gentlemen," he urged, "Ladies in the centre, Gents on the outside, forming two circles."

The band continued to play while the women turned to the left and the men to the right. Next they walked around in a circle until the music ceased and after coming to a halt, each person turned inwards, leaving a man facing a woman. Mack addressed the audience. "Introduce yourselves, then off we go!" The band played a Waltz, the music stopping halfway through, then the circles were formed again and the same procedure took place. A quickstep followed, and of course each lady had a different partner. Mack had a wealth of experience as an MC, so as expected the Paul Jones did the trick. The people obviously enjoyed themselves, and at five-thirty the tea-dance came to a close.

I dashed round to the betting shop just as it was about to close. My second selection, Wee Pedro, had won at 8-1. I carefully scanned the results board and my heart nearly missed a beat. Peter the Great had romped in at 4-1! To make my day complete, Peter and the Wolf came in first at even money. I could hardly believe my luck and realised that I had won a lot of money! The bookie asked me if I wouldn't mind coming back the next day to collect my winnings, because he had not had the opportunity to work the bet out, and they were just about to shut-up shop. I agreed , then rushed back to my lodgings to work the bet out. I came to £214 and 2 shillings (£214.10p), less betting tax (at that time 6d in the pound). The following morning I dashed down the betting-shop to collect my winnings. I had worked the bet out correctly, so the bookmaker grudgingly paid me out. That evening I treated the lads to a drink, at the same time wondering what had happened to change my luck!

One Sunday, Pete, Derek and I went down to the beach early and as it turned out to be extremely hot, spent most of that morning in the sea.

"A bit of a shortage of girls this year," Derek grumbled.

"Oh, I don't know about that," I replied, "I've seen one or two gorgeous ones around here."

Pete, being married, didn't enter into the conversation, but said abruptly, "You two should get married, not to each other I hasten to add, then you wouldn't need to be chasing after girls!"

"Old sourpuss!" Derek and I scoffed at him, splashing Pete with sea-water.

After a while we lay down on the sand, exhausted, then we three friends basked in the beautiful sunshine until lunchtime.

"Time for a beef-burger and a pint!" Pete shouted at us, and then "Wake up we can't lie here all day."

We changed, and then proceeded to the Merton Hotel for a drink and a bite to eat. As my friends and I entered the non-residents bar I was amazed to see Lottie.

'This is too much of a coincidence', I thought, 'It's been years'.

True enough, it had been a long time since Butlins, riding with Mrs Harris, and the 'accident'.

"Peter!" she screamed, rushing over to wear I stood.

After giving her a hug and a kiss, I turned to Pete and Derek.

"This is Lottie, who I've told you so much about."

"Pleased to meet you," they both said.

"What brings you to Jersey?" I asked.

"I might ask you the same thing," she answered.

"We're playing with the band at the West Park Pavilion," I went on, "And how about you?"

Lottie pointed to her two friends, "Helen, Jean and I are on holiday here for two weeks," she said.

After a pleasant evening, wandering around the bars and generally chatting, my two friends and I bade the girls goodnight. I did see Lottie twice more before she left the island but our 'old flame' had flickered and died out. Still, we parted good friends and I escorted her to the airport, where we said goodbye to one another.

The summer season in Jersey had come to an end, so I returned home to Neasden to live with my Mum and Dad. The following few months were very frustrating: Apart from a few 'gigs' I hardly received an engagement worth talking about. One day I saw an advert in the paper: 'Salesmen required for a Vacuum Cleaner Co. Commission only'. I applied for the position, which they gave to me on three months trial.

My first night as a 'tallyman' seemed quite interesting, although hard on the feet! The salesmen went out in a team each evening, the team consisting of six salesmen and a supervisor. The van stopped at a given point, and then the salesmen started to canvass for business. As soon as a householder showed interest, the supervisor had to be summoned to demonstrate the cleaner and push for a sale. I had knocked at some twenty doors before a lady said that she did need a new cleaner. I summoned Ginger the supervisor, then the demo began...

"Do you mind if I sprinkle some dust on your carpet, Madam?" Ginger asked.

"Er.... I don't know about that!" the prospective customer said, hesitantly.

Ginger took an over-flowing ashtray and emptied the contents onto the beautiful front-room carpet.

"Don't worry," Ginger reassured her, "We'll have this mess cleaned up in no time!"

He attached the suction head to the pipe and fixed them to the flying-saucer-shaped vacuum cleaner, finally plugging into the mains. An almighty bang greeted him and smoke bellowed out from the machine! Fortunately, Ginger carried a fire-extinguisher around with him, just in case. It didn't take long to curtail the smoke, but the front room had suffered. The neat pile of dust and cigarette ends was strewn across the room. The furniture had turned black and even the poor white Persian cat, had turned black. What a disaster! The lady screamed abuse at Ginger and me.

"Do you realise that all I have to clean up this mess is a dust pan and brush?"

By this time her husband had returned, and needless to say, the unfortunate pair of salesmen were cleaning and scrubbing, until the early hours of the following day!

"I can't understand it," Ginger had almost burst into tears, "I've been selling cleaners for this company for fifteen years, and this has never happened before!"

I remained with the vacuum cleaner company for three weeks, but the only person to buy one from me was – yes, you've guessed it – my Mum!

What would I do, what would become of me? I obviously did not have the talent (perhaps I should say 'gall') to be a salesman and apart from music I couldn't think of anything I wanted to do! I had reached the ripe old age of 22 and my ambition still eluded me. Each week, I bought the 'Melody Maker', the 'Musical Express' and the 'Stage'. I attended many auditions, wrote many letters trying everything that I could to obtain work as a musician.

It was at that time, that a well- known fixer and agent, Sid Jerome, put some work my way. He fixed the bands at the Dorchester, Hilton and many other large hotels in the West End of London. I started to become desperate, living at home with, at the most, two gigs a week and no prospects. Every Monday afternoon I took a bus to the West End, got off at Piccadilly Circus, then walked to Archer Street, the famous street adjacent to the Windmill Theatre ('We Never Closed!'), where musicians gathered to exchange telephone numbers and fix one another for 'gigs'.

After talking to numerous people, I decided to have a cup of coffee. As I walked into the café, I saw my Uncle Jim. Eleven years had elapsed since we had last met, but I recognised him straight away.

"Hello, Jim," I said, 'It has been a long while."

He looked at me for a few moments before answering.

"Hello, Peter," he said, "I didn't recognise you at first."

I just started to continue the conversation, but before I had the opportunity to speak, Jim got up from the chair.

"I'm sorry, Peter, but I have an appointment. Give my love to your Mum, Dad and Christine." With that, he held out his hand and said, "Here you are."

I looked at the coin he had given me – a two shilling piece. I handed it back to him and said indignantly, "Thanks all the same, but your need must be greater than mine!"

That turned out to be the last time that we ever met, which is rather tragic, but just one of those things!

By 1959 Mum, Dad and I were falling out more often than I care to remember, so I decided to find a flat and move away from home, yet again. I found a job as a salesman with a stationery company, in the heart of the City of London. Again it was on a commission-only basis, but with expenses plus a high rate of commission on sales, my take-home pay wasn't too bad. I found it extremely hard work, walking the streets of London and the suburbs, trying to sell typewriter carbon-paper, ribbons and stapling machines to people who didn't really want to buy. I had to climb hundreds of flights of stairs and tell many 'little white lies' to gain access to offices, in order to see the buyers.

My mother and father had been taken on as co-managers of The Castle pub in the City Road, Old Street, London and were doing fairly well. I went to see them from time to time, finding that I got on better with them now that we were living apart. After a few months, the pub had to be demolished to make way for new office blocks, so they took on another one, The White Hart at Stoke Newington in North London. Meanwhile, I still struggled with the stationery job (at the same time, still hoping to fulfil my ambition). I remained in the selling job until 1962 and by this time I hardly touched an instrument, having sold them to help to pay for rent and food – the last thing I wished to do, but I had to live.

In February 1962 I joined London Transport as a bus conductor; a far cry from my ambition to be a musician, but maybe one day... I worked as a London Transport bus conductor for two years, some weeks getting up at 4am and walking two miles to the garage, in all weathers. Sometimes I worked a 'spread-over' starting at 7am through until noon, breaking until 6pm, then working until midnight. On other occasions I worked the late shift from 4pm until midnight.

In 1964 I joined my mother and father, who were now managing Rayners Lane Tennis and Social Club in Middlesex. I changed jobs numerous times before starting a new career in the 'Betting Shop' business, working for George Mason.

In 1966, the World Cup finals were held in England. At that time, I belonged to the Middlesex Yeomanry (whilst they were still officially TA musicians). The band had been booked to play for the Lever Brothers Sports Day. Oddly enough that coincided with the day that the World Cup Final was staged at Wembley Stadium. England had reached a World Cup Final for the first time and their opponents were West Germany. The whole country, even those not normally football enthusiasts, were excited at the prospect. I too had looked forward to seeing 'The Match' and was disappointed to think that I would not be able to do so.

The band arrived at 1.30pm at Lever Brothers' playing fields. The track and field events were due to start at 2pm, so that gave the musicians half an hour in which to set up in one of the marquees. As my friends and I were wandering around we noticed that there were six of these large marquees; each had a TV set installed inside.

'Surely that's unusual for a sports day,' I thought, 'I wonder what those are for?'

The reason soon became clear; the World Cup Final! At 2pm the band started to play, and after 30 minutes (during which we had played light music) we began to play a selection of music from 'Call Me Madam'. Suddenly all the TV sets were switched on and before we were able to move out of the way, the marquee was swarming with people. Many of the music stands were sent flying and sheet music became strewn everywhere.

"That's it until half-time lads," the bandmaster said. "Enjoy the match."

It had become impossible to see the screen, so we wandered from one marquee to another until we found one that wasn't so densely populated. We were so engrossed in the game that when the half-time whistle blew we had forgotten that we were supposed to be playing!

Throughout the afternoon the track and field events took place as normal, even though the football match was being played at the same time. At the end of each race, the competitors wandered into one of the marquees for refreshments, then sat down to watch the match. All the eats and drinks were FOC, so everyone could just help themselves.

There was just one small snag with that – the alcoholic drinks were poured into bowl-shaped glasses, put onto trays, then laid out on the tables, that had been provided. Instead of separating the trays (or indeed if the whiskey and brandy had been put into different shaped glasses, it would have made more sense, but the whiskey and brandy had been placed side by side and in the same-shaped glasses. If anyone had looked closely, the difference would have been obvious, but as they were all chatting away and enjoying themselves everyone including myself were mixing their drinks, unintentionally!

During the half-time interval, the band played tunes from the musicals *Kismet* and *Carousel* and the ballet *Swan Lake*. I felt relieved that I didn't have a car at that time, because I had started to feel quite tipsy. The sheet music had started to become blurry, although it didn't really matter anyway, because once the second half had started, we would not be required to perform again. The whistle blew to signal the start of the second half, and we musicians sat down to watch it. I had considerable difficulty in keeping my eyes open, especially as the game went into extra time. England, of course, emerged the victor by four goals to two, thereby creating a piece of footballing history. Everyone went wild with delight, in fact the whole of England celebrated that night, and a few more nights after that! I couldn't remember the journey home. I could just about recall stepping into the coach, then the next thing I became aware of was Frank the solo cornettist shaking me.

"Hey, wake up Sleeping Beauty, you're home," he said.

I managed to drag myself up the stairs to the flat, flop into bed, then drifted away into an unconscious haze. Sunday had been and gone, but I didn't know anything about it. I had slept through until the time arrived to go to work on Monday morning. For the second time in my life I had awakened with a gigantic hangover.

'Still,' I thought, 'It had been worth it!'

Dad had returned to the music business and we were now all living together at Ruislip, Middlesex. My training as a betting shop assistant lasted six weeks, during which I travelled to Harrow and Wealdstone by bus, six days a week. My working hours were from 9am to 6pm. I had been trained to mark up the runners and riders on the board, taking bets, using the cash till, and learning all the racing terms and expressions. After my training they assigned me to my local betting shop at Ruislip Manor, only a few minutes walk from my home. On my first day at the shop, John the Manager greeted me.

"Welcome Pete, I know that we are going to hit it off, together!" My duties were to pin up the runners and riders from the daily newspapers and the *Sporting Life*, then mark up the 'whiteboard' using felt tip pens, ready for the results of the afternoon's racing. I had also to take bets and pay out the winners from previous days. It proved an extremely long and tiring working week!

Sometimes, if there was a big race such as the Grand National or the Derby, the shop would be full to capacity all day long, with punters placing bets in the morning and remaining for the rest of the day. The busiest day of the week was Saturday, with at least one greyhound meeting in the morning, covered by 'Extel' with commentary. During the week, when we were not quite so busy, John taught me how to settle bets.

The Middlesex Yeomanry TA Band had moved its headquarters, first to Harrow, then to Honeypot Lane, Kingsbury, where it remained until the re-organisation of the TA in 1967. The Band met each Thursday evening and Sunday morning to rehearse. It was quite a large band; twenty-five musicians in all. Luckily for me, I had been able to borrow a band instrument. Unfortunately for me, it turned out to be my old pet hate, the Eb clarinet, but it was better than no instrument at all. In the band there were, as usual, quite an assortment of people from different walks of life. I palled up with John, who would turn out to be the best friend I ever had. John played the trumpet and cornet (and was also quite a dab hand at the double string bass and piano accordion). He lived at Gerrards Cross, Buckinghamshire and drove a white Triumph Spitfire, which we travelled in quite a lot, as I didn't drive at that time.

We spent the last official TA Camp at Tilshead, Wiltshire, near to the famous ruins at Stonehenge. I used two of my three weeks annual holiday so that I could attend. We went together in John's car, having quite a breathtaking ride to the camp! As it would be the final engagement before we were to be disbanded, we were going to make the most of it. The barracks were similar to those at West Kirby, out in the middle of nowhere, windy and exceptionally cold. We two friends booked in at the guardroom, unloaded our gear, then entered the billet.

"God, what a dump!" John gasped.

"Seconded!" I agreed.

It looked like a typical Army billet, with one exception, it was filthy! The 'black-lead' boiler that stood in the centre of the room looked as if it hadn't been used for years.

"We certainly are going to have our work out cleaning up *this* place," I said.

"Thank goodness it's only for a fortnight," John answered.

The remainder of the band arrived soon afterwards, so we busied ourselves unpacking and generally cleaning up the billet. Soon the living quarters were 'spick and span' and even though it had been exceptionally hard graft we quite enjoyed ourselves (different from being in the Armed Forces!).

The first week was taken up by rehearsing for the Queen Mother's visit. The battalion was away on manoeuvres, so the band spent most of the time perfecting 'Handel's Fireworks Music', which was going to be used as the main theme for the military display in Her Majesty's honour. On the following Saturday, the halfway point of the fortnight's camp, we had a full dress rehearsal. Naturally, it rained; wasn't that always the case? After everyone had spent hours and hours 'bulling' their uniforms, down it came! There was one consolation for us; we were allowed to play under a marquee.

The rehearsal commenced at 0930 hours and continued, with a break for lunch, then again for dinner, until 2230 hours. The Saracen tanks lined up on the brow of the hill, then as the strains of Handel's Firework Music filled the air, the tanks moved in formation downhill. That manoeuvre alone had to be repeated at least one hundred times. The CO would not be satisfied until all the vehicles were perfectly synchronised. At one stage of the proceedings the CO rushed over to the marquee and complained to the bandmaster that the music had been played too slowly. By this time darkness had fallen, so we could hardly see our music. My fingers were frozen with the cold, and to make matters worse, being in the front row of the band, I had to suffer the drips from the roof of the tent and felt like a 'drowned rat'. At long last, the officer was satisfied and the Regiment could be dismissed.

The next day being Sunday, John a few others and I decided to have a day out. After the early morning Church Parade we jumped into cars and went to Salisbury. Unfortunately, I hadn't learned to drive, so it fell upon poor old John to do the honours.

"I really must take driving lessons, mate," I said apologetically.

"You can get those free in the TA," John replied. "Inquire when we get back home."

I decided to do just that. We arrived at Salisbury just after 1100 hours. The rest of the lads were standing outside the great cathedral, waiting for us. After being shown around the cathedral, the lads went to see the ruins at Stonehenge, then we finished our day by visiting Bath.

We spent the second week at camp, rehearsing with the regiment, in readiness for the Queen Mother's visit. We musicians passed our evenings either in the NAAFI or down at the local pub. One evening my friends and I were returning from a visit to the 'local' and, as it was a particularly dark night, with no moon, stars or any street lighting to guide us up the long winding lane back to camp, we felt as a blind person might feel, quite helpless! We were keeping as close as possible to one another when I slipped, bringing John down with me. The others followed, slipping and sliding, falling down like ninepins. We had wandered into a cow field and were plastered with thick mud and sludge. As we entered the billet, there were cries of, "Look out, the mud larks are here!" from the others.

"Very funny!" I retorted.

"Oh come on, just have a look at yourselves," someone shouted out at us.

We certainly did look a sight, and one look in the mirror made me explode with laughter. In the end we all saw the funny side of it.

The display went extremely well and the Queen Mother congratulated everyone, pausing to speak to one or two members of the band. She even spoke to me, which did give me a thrill I must admit!

I returned to work, feeling more contented than I had felt in months. At least I had been playing again, also mixing with musicians once more. The first day back at work felt a little strange, but it always does so after a long break. John asked me if I had enjoyed myself.

"I had a great time," I answered, then related some of the things that had happened.

In the afternoon, the shop had become full to capacity. One of the regulars, a pensioner, came up to the counter.

"I'll just have my usual, son," he said, passing the bet to me.

I felt sorry for the old man, 'I do wish that old people wouldn't bet', I thought. 'I'm sure they can't afford it'.

The months passed by, I still liked to have an occasional bet, but not being allowed to bet in my own shop, I placed my wagers at Alexander's at Ruislip. One morning, I was casting my eyes over the runners and riders at Alex's, when Eddie, one of the partners spoke to me.

"How would you like to work for us? He asked.

"It would depend on the wages, Eddie," I replied.

After discussing the money and realising that the prospects were better, I decided to change jobs.

By now Mum and Dad had made yet another move and were managing Uxbridge Golf Club. As the Betting Shop was only twenty minutes walk away, I moved in with them. The year was 1968 and I still worked at Alex's during the day, and playing with the ex-TA band some evenings (the Middx.-Yeomanry had not disbanded, even though they were no longer an official TA Band) and Colonel Bill, who knew nothing about music, but had plenty of money, decided to take the band under his wing. We assumed a new title, 'The Middlesex Yeomanry Old Comrades Band'. That did not mean to say that all the members were old people, just a title to enable the musicians to wear the same uniform, but having an old comrades badge as an insignia.

The HQ of the Old Comrades Band was situated at Horn Lane, Acton, London. Most of the original members had remained, but one or two had moved on to other bands. I played the Eb clarinet with the band, the Bb clarinet with the Royal Yeomanry at Chancery Lane, London and, to top it all, I also played with the British Legion at Norbury, SW London. From not playing at all, I now played with at least three bands!

In 1970 I met my future wife, Pauline. At that time I still lived with my parents at the Golf Club, but had changed Turf Accountants to Percy Baker's at Uxbridge. I hadn't been to the Wembley Town Hall for years, but at the suggestion of my good friend John, we went on Saturday 6th June (my sister Christine's birthday). The dance hall was extremely large, but although there were tables surrounding the dance floor, my friend and I had to stand. The ballroom had filled up early and there wasn't a lot of space to dance comfortably.

"There are two girls sitting on their own," John said.

I looked over to where they were sitting.

"Come on then," I answered.

John headed directly for Pauline, then asked her to dance. I took her sister Rose onto the dance-floor. After the selection of quicksteps I thanked Rose, then returned to where John stood.

"How was your dance, Peter? he asked me.

"Quite nice," I said, "but she is rather quiet."

"That's a coincidence," John went on, "mine is the same."

We decided to change partners for the next dance, the band started to play a Samba – Tico-Tico (one of my favourites) – and after talking to her for only five minutes, I knew that Pauline was the girl for me.

Over the next few months Pauline and I met once every week, going for long walks – sometimes strolling by the Welsh Harp Lake at Neasden and sometimes walking over to Harrow-on-the-Hill. Although she didn't talk a lot, we got along exceptionally well. She has always been a really private person; kind, considerate and all-in-all, just the sort of person I would wish to spend the rest of my life with. Pauline came from a large family. She lived with her mother and father at Neasden, NW London. She had two brothers living at home and another who was married. She also had four sisters living at home. It was strange, because I had lived at Neasden before moving to Uxbridge. That I should go to Wembley to meet her surely must have been fate, because she had never been to Wembley Town Hall before.

I spent Christmas 1970 with Pauline and her family, by whom I had been accepted with open arms. Christmas at her home was really exciting, I had never spent a Yuletide quite like it before, the house being full of people all over the holiday. The problem with Pauline's Mum was that she would insist on filling me up with food. No sooner had I walked into the house than a sandwich and a cup of tea were thrust into my hands. As I had not been accustomed to eating like that, I began to put on weight.

By May 1971 both Pauline and I had passed our driving tests (on the first attempt!) Mum had bought an Austin Mini van cheaply from a salesman who had to go abroad. As he played golf at the club regularly, he asked Mum if she happened to know anyone who would like to buy his van.

"That would be ideal for my son, as he has just passed his driving test," she told him.

The van was only two years old and at £150 appeared to be a genuine bargain. I lived to regret having bought the vehicle, however, but at the time I found it useful and I felt grateful to my Mum for lending me £50 to put toward the purchase.

By February 1971, Pauline and I had been going together for 8 months. Although neither of us had any previous intention of getting married, I realised that I loved her more than anything or anyone in the world. I had always been made welcome at her house and Pauline's Dad helped me to maintain the van. We agreed to get married in October of that year, but before that could happen I was involved in an accident, which nearly cost me my life and completely wrecked the 'Mini'...

The Middlesex Yeomanry 'Old Comrades' Band had an engagement at the Duke of York's Barracks, Chelsea. The parade commemorated 'Lafone Day', a First World War battle celebrated annually by the Army. In the evening I was driving home, over Hammersmith flyover, when suddenly a lorry travelling in the opposite direction, went out of control. The next moment I could feel the mini-van spinning around in circles. I sat there in a painful haze. I could literally see stars, and my right arm and sides were giving me a lot of pain.

"Are you alright?" a voice from the distance enquired.

"Yes, I think so," I managed to mumble, "but there is something wrong with my side and right arm…"

Then I lost consciousness once more.

I awakened to find myself lying on a bed in the hospital. There were two policemen standing by the bedside.

"How are you feeling now?" the taller of the two asked.

I ached, but apart from that, I didn't feel too bad. I was really upset to learn that the van was a write-off. The police towed it away to the accident repair centre, but it would soon end up in the scrap-yard.

The two bobbies were exceptionally kind. After phoning my mum, they actually drove me to the Golf Club to find a very relieved Rachel waiting there for me. Some weeks later, they called back to see how I had progressed.

In October 1971, Pauline and I were married in the Willesden Registry Office. She, naturally, had wished for a big wedding in the church, but I didn't want all the pomp and ceremony that it would entail. Pauline's Mum and Dad had laid out a wonderful spread for us and I felt happier than at any other time in my life.

I would never be lonely again, but there was just one thing missing, my music. I still had that frustrated feeling every time I thought about it, even though I belonged to three semi-professional bands at that time. I longed to play professionally again, because job-wise I had been going through an exceptionally bad patch – three months with Godfrey Davis, the Ford dealers; four and a half years with Alacra, printers and stationers; and eighteen months with Maxlove, printers at Neasden. I had been made redundant twice, but Pauline stood by my side through it all.

Pauline and I were buying a flat at Harlesden, London NW10 and while we were living there, Debbie, our first child came into the world. Deborah Lorraine arrived on the scene on 3rd January 1976 and both Pauline and myself were overjoyed about the event. She weighed 6lbs 7ozs and had the most jovial and pleasant nature.

I rejoined the TA in May 1976 with the Inns of Court Royal Yeomanry Band, which was based at Chancery Lane, London WC1 and used to rehearse every Wednesday evening. In comparison with all the other bands I had played with, the Yeomanry was not a big outfit. It consisted of only four clarinets, two cornets, one trombone, alto sax, tenor sax, French horn and percussion. Musically, they performed extremely well, but were not able to do marching displays due to lack of numbers.

In the summer of 1977 the band spent their camp at Castlemartin in Pembrokeshire. I took Pauline and baby Debbie with me, also Pauline's sister Rose, to keep them company while I performed my duties. We rented a caravan at Lydsterp Haven, Tenby. We picked up Pauline's sister, then proceeded to Wales. The drive, although rather long, took us through beautiful parts of England and Wales, and as we were able to share the driving, it was not too tiring. We stopped a few times along the way, to allow everyone to stretch their legs. Pauline had made a picnic lunch of salad, bread rolls, cake and a flask of coffee, so the journey turned out to be extremely pleasant.

On arrival at Lydstep Haven, we booked in and were then shown to our caravan. It turned out to be a two-berth accommodation, allowing Rose to sleep in one, leaving me and the other two in the other. I had to report to the camp that evening, so I changed into uniform, climbed into the Hillman Imp and drove off. I assured my wife that I would not be late, as I only had to report to the guardhouse, then would be free until the following Monday morning. I arrived at the TA barracks just ahead of the rest of the band. The Bandmaster arrived next.

"Hello Peter, enjoy your journey?"

"Yes thanks, Sir," I replied, "very Pleasant!"

Frank had a reasonably easy-going nature and everyone liked and respected him. At last all the band had arrived and the Band Sergeant addressed us.

"I will sign you all in, then you are free to do as you please until Monday morning at 0700 sharp, and then there will be a rehearsal at 0900 in the gymnasium."

I would be the only one living out, so Ron gave me a whole list of engagements for the duration of our stay at camp, just in case anything prevented me from arriving at the camp the following Monday. The journey from Pembroke to Lydstep took roughly thirty minutes by car, and as there were some particularly nasty bends to negotiate, I didn't dare to drive too quickly. I arrived back at the caravan site at tea-time, changed back into 'civvies', and relaxed with my family. Sitting by the window of the caravan, watching the waves rolling in, the seagulls diving for fish, and the children playing on the beach, made me feel relaxed and at peace with the world!.

The following morning, I woke up early, filled the plastic water bottle with fresh water from the pump, then returned to the caravan. The sun shone, but a severe, gusty wind made my face tingle. After breakfast, we climbed into the Hillman Imp and drove to Tenby – quite a large town with plenty of shops for the girls to browse around. The market had a fine selection of fresh meat and vegetables, so Pauline stocked up for a couple of days, as the caravan had a mini-fridge that would keep the food fresh. The caravan site had its own shop, which supplied most of the campers needs, but it appeared to be extremely expensive. The only means of recreation was a table-tennis room and a clubhouse. The table-tennis room had two full-sized tables and some cheap bats, but the balls had to be supplied by the user. At that time

I only played 'ping-pong', but had a pleasant surprise to learn that Pauline had become an accomplished 'table-tennis' player. The clubhouse had two bars and a hall, mainly accommodating 'bingo'.

After a weekend of swimming and sightseeing, I reported to Castle Martin for duty. In the past, the TA Bands had gone away to camp for two weeks, but under the new re-organisation rules, this had been cut to one.

At 0830 hrs the Band formed up for rehearsal in the NAAFI canteen.

"On Saturday evening, we will be marching and playing on the Battlements of Pembroke Castle," Frank told us, then continued. "The programme will be as follows: The Farmers Boy (Regimental March of the Royal Yeomanry), followed by the William Tell Overture. After that I will make my welcoming speech to the audience, crack a few jokes, then we will continue playing with the Planets Suite by Gustav Holtz, a Glen Miller selection, then break for fifteen minutes. There will be beer and sandwiches provided during the interval."

Frank paused for a while then said, "Have a smoke lads, while we are discussing the programme."

I thought that it seemed quite a pleasant programme, also particularly suitable for the occasion. The Bandmaster continued with his plans for the programme. "After the interval we will continue with Wind in the Wood (a special arrangement featuring the clarinet section, accompanied by the rest of the band) and next a selection of marches, then the Regimental March to finish."

The week passed by really quickly as I travelled to Castle Martin by car each day, and most days I arrived back at the caravan by 1400 hrs. One evening the band played for the Officers' Mess Dinner, but apart from that and the Saturday Evening Concert at Pembroke Castle, the evenings were free.

Saturday arrived, bringing with it a slight problem: My family and I had to vacate the caravan by 0900, so we had to pack up our belongings and load them into the car. That meant tat we had to find somewhere to go for the remainder of the day. It had been an extremely enjoyable week and luckily the band did not have too many commitments, so I had plenty of free time for my family.

The Royal Yeomanry band lined up in the High Street of Pembroke, then marched through the town to the castle. Although lacking in numbers, we provided a smart display of marching and playing. The crowds that had gathered on both sides of the High Street, clapped and cheered. At last the Band reached Pembroke Castle, broke ranks, then re-assembled in readiness for the performance on the battlements. A large audience had gathered to listen to the band and they were well rewarded. They showed their appreciation in the usual way.

During the year 1977, I took a Government Training Course in Typing, Shorthand and Audio, because I still struggled as a musician, I thought it best to achieve further skills in the clerical field. I had been to the Department of Employment and had been offered a choice of two training courses, the options being a course in bricklaying or the one in clerical skills. I chose the latter.

It certainly did not seem to be the best time to enter into new fields. The flat in Harlesden had a leaking roof and a resident mouse! My sleeping pattern had become erratic, mind you, I laugh now when I think of it! Dashing around with buckets, whenever it rained did not seem very funny. Still, life had to go on, so I boarded the tube and headed for Liverpool Street Station.

The Dynamic School of Typing, Shorthand and Audio appeared to be well organised. Each lesson had been particularly prepared, to enable the student to get the most out of the course. I enjoyed my three months there, even though I turned out to be the only male amongst a dozen females. My first day was unusual to say the least, but I soon became used to the routine. I took my seat (a thorn amongst the roses!) as Mr Hughes welcomed the students.

"Good-morning students, please take your seats as quickly as possible, thank you."

We were issued with books: a shorthand notepad, a textbook to explain all the signs and abbreviations, and finally a Typewriter Instruction Manual. The School used both kinds of machine, manual and electric, so the students were to be trained on each. After the introductory speech, the students were transferred to another room, containing benches, typists stools and typewriters. I sat down in front of my old Olympia Manual Typewriter and gazed at the screen in front of me. There, projected onto it, was a picture of a typewriter. As soon as everyone had taken their seats, Mr Hughes commenced the lesson.

"Put on your earphones, students," he said, then, "switch on your tapes and obey the instructions."

The tune I heard would be buzzing around in my head for the next three months, a catchy Latin-American number, the title of which escaped me, but I knew it well. After the introductory melody, the instructor's voice issued the commands.

"Good-morning everyone, and welcome to the Dynamic School of Typing, Shorthand and Audio. The Tune you have just heard will be the introduction to each lesson. Let's begin… Look at the keyboard in front of you, then place both of your hands onto it, making sure that the RH index finger is placed on to the letter J, and the LH index finger is on F. Keep your eyes fixed on the screen in front of you, then strike the F key, next the J key. Repeat this movement, still keeping your eyes on the screen, until I tell you to stop."

The instruction tape lasted for thirty minutes. At the end of it, the signature tune played once more to indicate the end of the lesson.

I decided to compose a song dedicated to my daughter Debbie, who had almost reached her first birthday. I remembered how, when I tried desperately hard to practise, she used to call out, "Ma-ma, Ma-ma," making it difficult for me to concentrate.

At that time, I didn't possess a piano or a guitar to enable me to work out the chord progressions. I composed the melody on my clarinet, writing it down on manuscript paper. Next I composed the lyrics to fit the tune. A light, bouncy song, but if I had aspirations of it becoming a hit, I would be bitterly disappointed. I worked for hour after hour at that song. 'At least', I thought, 'Even if it doesn't make the charts, Debbie will have a song to remember me by'.

The three months training at the Typing School had reached its conclusion and I had received a diploma, showing that I had achieved an excellent standard in all three aspects of the course: 60 words per minute on the manual t/w, 70 wpm on the electric t/w and the same for audio. I hoped that, with my knowledge of French, I would be able to establish myself in remunerative employment.

For my birthday, Pauline treated me to a guitar; I had never played the instrument before, but was sure that, with practise, I could become proficient on it. This would also give me the opportunity, to complete the song for Debbie.

I went to the Department of Employment every day, wrote letters applying for jobs, also making numerous telephone calls, but without success. One day, the clerk at the Exchange gave me an introduction card for a transport company based at Hendon in North West London; they needed a clerk/typist. Although the salary did not seem too inviting, I needed a job, so I climbed into the Hillman Imp and made my way to the interview.

The Manager greeted me with, "I know I shouldn't be saying this to you, but I really would have preferred a girl…" (at that time the Sex Discrimination Act did exist). He continued, "You will see why, when I tell you what Anne is doing at the present. She makes the tea and runs errands in addition to her clerical duties. Can you see yourself doing those things?"

"I will do my best," I answered.

On the following Monday morning, I reported for work and Mr Smith introduced me to the long-distance lorry drivers.

"This is Peter, who is taking over from Anne," he told them.

They all welcomed me, but I did receive some quizzical looks. After a couple of months of routine typing and general clerical work, I found myself settling in quite well. I had become used to cries of 'take a letter Miss Bradbury' from the lorry drivers. In fact, they made me laugh and really were a likeable crowd. One morning as I sat at my typewriter, the telephone rang. I picked up the receiver, "Good-morning, can I help you?" I asked.

"Is that Peter Bradbury?" the voice at the other end of the line enquired.

"Yes," I replied, "To Whom am I speaking?"

"It's Matt, I used to play the euphonium with the Middlesex Yeomanry Band."

I felt slightly puzzled, I did remember Matt, but wondered why he should be phoning me.

"I phoned your Dad, and he gave your works phone number to me," Matt continued, "Are you available for two weeks playing at Barry in Wales?"

I couldn't believe what I had heard.

"Yes," I replied, "I certainly am available," forgetting for the moment the job I had to do, "What kind of music is it Matt?"

"I run a Tyrolean Group – tenor sax, brass bass, trombone and bass guitar," Matt told me. "The alto sax/clarinet player is not available, hence I asked around, and you were recommended to me."

I told a little white lie to my manager, saying that I had previously booked two weeks holiday. To my surprise he agreed, but added that I would have to forfeit two weeks pay. I felt highly delighted. Thank goodness I would have an opportunity to play professionally, be it only for two weeks. 'After all, who knows what might come of it?' I thought.

At long last, after what seemed like an eternity, the time arrived for my trip to Barry. The 350-mile drive didn't take too long and I soon arrived at my destination. I spent the first week at a lodging house, but for the second week I stayed at a Three Star Hotel, close to the Dance Hall where I would be working. The band uniform appeared to be quite quaint: a Tyrolean hat, complete with feather, white shirt and black 'dickie-bow', flower-patterned braces, and to complete the outfit, long yellow socks pulled over black trousers (no shorts, unfortunately).

There were two performances daily – a matinee in the afternoon and a show in the evening. While performing on stage, each member of the band was given a 'stein' to drink German beer from. It should have been for effect only, but each time I emptied mine, someone promptly refilled it. Although tasting like lemonade, it was far from that, as I soon found out! The band lined up in the town, ready for the short march to the ballroom. We marched off to the famous Radeszki March (Ride of the Valkeries), then marched into the hall, up the steps and onto the stage. I had known Alan, the tenor saxophonist, previously, we had played together with the Royal British Legion Band at Norbury. Alan really was a proficient musician and his rendering of 'Yakkety-Sax' sounded marvellous.

The music made everyone want to get up and dance, and although they were obviously enjoying themselves, due to the fact there were no set dances for the Alpine-type music, so they had to content themselves by jigging and jumping up and down. For the greater part of the evening, the band played tunes for ballroom dancing, but alternated with the Tyrolean tunes. During the interval, the tuba player and the trombonist marched up and down the hall, wearing German Army steel helmets and performed the 'goose step', strutting along to the laughter of the audience.

The German beer had begun to get the better of me and towards the end of the evening I felt a little giddy. After the dance, I walked back to my lodgings, and after a few moments the fresh air cleared my head. The following morning I woke up with a 'king-size' headache and as I looked at my watch thought 'Good heavens, just look at the time it's 11.30 already I must get up! That simple operation did not seem as easy as I first thought. As I attempted to stand up, my legs gave way beneath me. I hauled myself up, staggered to the window, and opened the curtains. The sun dazzled me. 'Oh I do feel ill' I thought. Suddenly, there came a knock on the door and a tiny voice called out.

"Can I come in, sir?"

"Yes," I answered shakily, "but do it quietly please."

The maid entered the room.

"There's a nice cup of tea for you," she said.

"Thank-you, it's just what I need," I said gratefully.

After drinking the tea, I felt much better, then dressed and went for a walk along the cliffs. After a while, the others joined me and we went for a swim and, feeling refreshed after the dip, I realised that I felt hungry, so I made my way back to my lodgings for lunch. The band formed up for the afternoon session, then marched into the ballroom. The steins had been filled up and carefully placed onto the stage and Matt faced the audience.

"Lift up your Steins mein Herrs und Herrens," he addressed them then continued, "We will now play for you the famous drinking song 'Ein Prosit'. Please sing along with us."

I had painful memories of that song, when John and I visited the German Beer Kellers in the West End of London. By the end of the first week in Barry, I had learned that if I wished to remain sober, I would have to make one stein of beer last throughout the performance. I transferred from my lodgings to a three-star hotel and the difference surprised me. In my room, every conceivable convenience came to hand – washbasin, bath, shower, television and radio.

The second week brought a near crisis for me. My eyes had been playing me up quite a lot of late and I had to wear reading glasses. One evening during the performance I experienced some difficulty seeing the music. The band were playing a piece I did not know. The lights were down low and due to the fact that I had to read from an old march card, I felt myself squinting. In between numbers Alan made a remark that infuriated me.

"You made a right mess of that last piece, I should cut down on the German beer if I was you, Pete!" he said sarcastically.

"The light is bad and my eyes seem to be playing me up," I snapped back at him, feeling hurt by that remark.

That led to quite a heated argument between us. Luckily, the interval intervened, so the band left the stage to eat the meal that had been provided for us.

"What's up with you two?" Matt demanded angrily.

"Sorry," I said, "it was unprofessional conduct."

"I agree," Alan joined in. "Sorry Matt."

He didn't apologise to me though, which made me feel worse than I did before. Fortunately for the two of us, the people were enjoying themselves so much that nobody noticed anything untoward had occurred. I decided to forget all about the incident and put it down to 'just one of those things'. The remainder of the week passed without a hitch, but as I got prepared to leave Barry, I asked Matt if there would be a chance of playing with the band permanently.

"Sorry, Peter," Matt replied, "our resident sax and clarinet player will be back with us next week... but I'll let you know if anything crops up."

I thanked him and went on my way.

Pauline and I were both getting tired of the aggravation with the flat and wished to sell up and buy a house, but who would want to buy a flat with a leaking roof and a resident mouse? Although we were purchasing the property form the GLC, the roof came under the jurisdiction of the landlord. At last, after months of arguments and discussions, the agents for the landowners agreed to tarmac the roof. They did this, only after I had been to the Citizens Advice Bureau, who put pressure on the agents. At that time a government scheme existed to help people purchase property, providing the buyer held a job in that area. I applied for a job in Milton Keynes and at the same time, Pauline and I went house hunting in that area.

By 1977, the house-building programme in the Milton Keynes area had become extensive. Pauline, baby Debbie and I went by car to see the new homes. We had approached the agents and the builders, but decided to see the properties for ourselves. We wanted to see the style of the houses that were being erected.

"I don't think much of the new style of houses that are being built here in Milton Keynes," Pauline said.

"Neither do I," I agreed, "They are a peculiar shape, also they seem to overdo the 'red brick' effect, a really deep colour and quite eye dazzling!"

We were watching the workmen on the site and overhearing our remarks one of the men said, "Why don't you take a trip to Newport Pagnell, you will prefer the houses there?"

After heeding the workman's advice, we decided to go in for one of the houses at Newport Pagnell. The flat at Harlesden (after having the roof fixed), did appear to be in a good state of repair, so we managed to sell up and move. It was 1978 before we finally moved into the house, then unfortunately for me, I would have to travel to work in London by car every day, for the following eighteen months. Three months prior to moving to Newport Pagnell I had transferred to another TA Band at Reading, Berks. I would be going away to camp twice more with the band, before finishing with the TA completely. In September 1978, I packed my kitbag, gathered my instruments and uniforms, then made my way to Kneller Hall School of Music at Slough.

The musicians (although very smart and musically proficient), were due for a shock during the week's camp at Kneller Hall. I had been used to 'bull' in the RAF and to a certain degree in the TA also, but at the Army School of Music the discipline was excessive. Even though we were only part-time soldiers/musicians, we came under the jurisdiction of the army and had to accept the discipline (however severe) without question. Shock number one came on the first day. We were aroused by reveille at 0530 hours, breakfast parade followed at 0630, which included being marched in formation to the cookhouse. Billet Inspection at 0730 (beds had to be made up military-style), 0830 the

Bandmaster and Band Sergeant came into the billet, giving out orders for the day.

"Listen in lads!" Ron said. "The Director of Music, Kneller Hall, has instructed me to tell you that there will be two hours marching drill each day. I know that it seems like an imposition, but let's face it, we do need it."

The news wasn't very well received, but true to the general spirit of the band, nobody complained.

The band's first rehearsal took place in 'the balloon'. Apparently it would be only a temporary accommodation, not shaped like a balloon, but dome-shaped and kept upright by a flow of air. The acoustics were not all that good, but due to a lack of room space at the school, the only answer, at that time, would be a temporary rehearsal room. It felt quite eerie, sitting there with the wind making 'the balloon' flap about. 'Rather claustrophobic', I thought, 'I hope it's secure!' Apparently there had been an incident, in which the balloon had collapsed, but nobody had been seriously hurt.

We finished rehearsing at 10.00 hours, walked out of the confines of the school, then wandered down to the local coffee shop for our break. After half of an hour we returned to duty, then formed up in preparation for the marching drill. The Drill Sergeant stood looking at the band for a few moments, jumped to attention, then marched smartly to where Frank stood. He stamped his feet together and whipped up a very smart salute.

"Sir!" he bellowed, "Permission to take your men for drill, Sir!"

Poor Frank nearly fell over; it had been many years since he had heard a Drill Instructor use his lungs to their full extent.

"Carry on Sergeant," he replied, returning the salute.

Memories of West Kirby flooded back… of 'Bulldog' and 'Basher' yelling, the 'Birk' wiping his wet fingers along the top of the lockers, Rick…

"Hey you!" the voice shook me out of my reverie, "Stop day-dreaming and get fell in!"

I jumped to attention, then lined up with the others.

"First of all, we will be marching without instruments, then afterwards with them," the DI told us.

The band marched up and down the 'square' with the Bandmaster at the head and the Band Sergeant bringing up the rear. The DI marched alongside the columns, giving out his instructions, deafening everybody.

"Left, right, left, right, le…ft," he ordered. "Watch the dressing, it's lousy!" he continued, "I wish I had you for a few weeks. You would soon smarten up!" Most of us were ex-servicemen, but there were one or two that had not been. After twenty minutes, the sergeant brought the band to a halt, then called the inexperienced ones out of the line.

"The rest of you can take five," he said, "I shall have to give some individual attention to these people, who have obviously never marched before."

After two hours of marching, counter-marching and performing other drill movements, we were exhausted.

"Be back at the balloon at 1400 hrs." Frank told us, then, "band dismiss."

Lunchtime had arrived, so the rest of the band and I headed for the cookhouse. The meal turned out to be quite reasonable. I had a salad, followed by fruit and custard, then went for a stroll by myself. Once again, the afternoon rehearsal took place in the Balloon. Frank climbed onto the rostrum and gave out a few titbits of information.

"We will have a short rehearsal, because I don't know about you lot, but I am worn out already. You will be free until tomorrow morning, but as there is a big day ahead, I suggest that you all get an early night."

After the evening meal I, Corporal Bradbury (note the new title), called the musicians to gather around me.

"Is anyone interested in forming a Dance Band? I have bought a library, admittedly it is fairly old material, but I thought it would make a pleasant change from the straight stuff."

They received the suggestion eagerly, so the Hatters Dance Band was born: two alto saxes, piano, bass, drums, two tenor saxes, two trumpets, one baritone sax and two trombones.

The line-up wasn't quite complete, but with special arrangements it should work out reasonably well. We decided (with the Bandmaster's permission) to have a daily rehearsal. Finally, after a game of snooker and a couple of pints of beer, we retired to bed.

The following day, the routine took the same pattern, except the rehearsal, which took place on the open-air concert stand. The TA Band intermingled with the Kneller Hall School of Music military band, to rehearse for a Grand Concert on the Saturday evening. It took place on a once a month basis, with invited guests from all parts of the British Isles. I settled down on the solo Bb clarinet stand, with my counterparts from the school. The Director of Music climbed onto the rostrum and the band rose from their seats.

"Be seated, Gentlemen," he said, "First, let us welcome into our ranks the band of the 2nd Wessex, late Bucks, Berks and Oxon. I hope that they are enjoying their short stay with us."

The rehearsal lasted for one hour, a short tea break, then continued until lunchtime. In the afternoon, the musicians were yet again made to go through the ordeal of two hours marching drill. After a break in which to get back our breath, Frank told me that I could, if I wished, rehearse the Dance band. One of the Students rehearsal rooms became available, so the Hatters, including myself, set up. I felt slightly nervous, not that I didn't know how to rehearse a band, but it was the first time I had run a large band of my very own.

"We'll have the five saxes in the front row," I began, "Then the two trumpets just behind to the left and the two trombones to the right, drums in the centre at the back and string bass in between the drums and piano."

The only foreseeable snag (as far as I could tell) could be the Bandmaster. Frank had offered to play the piano, but although I had the full responsibility for the running of the Dance Band, Frank had already started to interfere.

"I'm not keen on the set-up," he said.

I knew that if I wished to maintain control, I would have to put my foot down.

"With all due respect Frank," I said, "If I am going to organise this Dance Band, I would prefer to do it my own way."

"Carry on, Peter, Frank urged me, "I won't interfere!"

It looked like being a difficult enough task to knock the music into shape, without someone trying to tell me how to do it.

"Let's have a Bb concert from the piano, please," I asked Frank. Finally, after the tuning had been synchronised, the rehearsal commenced.

"Can we have a look at the 'Jimmy Lally' arrangement of 'South of the Border' (Down Mexico Way)" I said.

"That's a bit 'Old Hat', isn't it?" Frank had started to interrupt... "Oops sorry Peter, please continue."

I realised that I had made my point, and carried on with the rehearsal. Although an old tune, that Latin-American melody, when well played, sounded extremely pleasant indeed. It took hours of rehearsing each section separately, going over each individual's difficult part, exhausted us all but we were having fun, that was the main thing.

As we were rehearsing, the Regimental Sergeant Major of the School of Music knocked and then entered the room.

"That sounds nice. A bit rough round the edges, but pleasant. Even made me feel like dancing."

"Thank-you, Sir," I said, accepting the compliment, also the criticism.

"Haven't you got anything more up-to-date than Jimmy Lally?" The RSM enquired.

"It is my own library sir, better than no music at all, at least, to start off the band with," I replied.

"Quite true," the RSM agreed.

Eventually, after hours of rehearsals, the Hatters Dance Band sounded ready for engagements. There were almost one hundred numbers in my dance band library. That should be enough to keep us going for a while, at least until I could afford to buy some more modern music.

Saturday arrived and the musicians spent a lot of time, preparing for the evening concert. Luckily, the weather had been kind to us, a sunny day, just the sort of temperature that we would have wished for, making conditions ideal for the performance. Admission to the show had to be by programme only, and as five hundred had been sold, it looked like being a Full House.

A one-hundred strong Military Band adorned the concert stage. The audience streamed in, then at eight o'clock the performance started. The overture 'Pomp and Circumstance' held the audience spellbound. At the end of the piece of music, the Conductor turned to the audience and saluted the tumultuous applause. The next piece, 'Toreador', from Bizet's Opera *Carmen* had been especially arranged by one of the students. The evening continued, with a varied selection of music, much to the delight of everyone listening.

The next day, the musicians packed ready for the long drive home. Even though I had only been separated from my wife and daughter for one week, I could hardly wait to get home to them.

By May that year, I had been travelling backwards and forwards to London, for five months. The job at Associated Automation Engineering had been taking a lot out of me. Although tiring, the work seemed quite varied and interesting, but with a journey of one hundred miles a day, I started to feel the pressure. I had been hired as a Progress Chaser, which entailed being at work by 7am, so I had to leave home at 5.30. On arrival, I had to sort out my paperwork from the previous day, then find a labourer to help me move cases of pressings from workshop to treatment centre. The company manufactured 'relays' and, being part of the GEC Group, provided me with enough work to keep me fully occupied. I had worked for the company for over a year, but prior to our move to Newport Pagnell, I had lived just ten minutes walk away.

The 2nd Wessex Band played for many functions, as had the previous bands that I had belonged to. In addition to driving seventy-six miles each way to Reading on a Tuesday evening for rehearsal, I had to travel at least that distance for every engagement. I got on very well with the other musicians, and it had been the first time that my talents had been fully appreciated. I kept the Dance Band going, which improved with each rehearsal.

As previously mentioned, I had been promoted to corporal, not that I worshipped power, but for one thing, it increased my TA allowance, and for another, as the solo clarinettist, gave me recognition of my position.

1979 turned out to be a tragic year for me. I had been dashing about from one part of the trading estate to the other when I heard my name being called out over the 'Tannoy' system…

"Will Peter Bradbury please return to the Production Office, where an urgent telephone call is awaiting him"

My heart began to thump. 'What on earth can that be about?' I thought. I rushed back to the office where Len the Production Control Manager, stood waiting for me. He handed the telephone receiver to me.

"Hello, who's speaking?" I enquired.

Pauline's Mum had called me, and she sounded distressed.

"I've just had a call from your Dad, dear, apparently, your Mum is seriously ill in hospital!"

Len gave me the rest of the day off, so after letting Pauline know what had happened, I dashed to the hospital at Northwood Hills, where they allowed me to see my Mum. Being under sedation, Rachel didn't recognise me, and I certainly did not recognise her! Her face had a yellow hue, almost like an egg yolk. One week later Mum passed away. Pauline, Dad and Christine and her husband Faico, were present at her cremation. Her ashes were scattered to the wind, leaving Dad heartbroken and me, well, we never had been close, but I felt an emptiness in the pit of my stomach, as if something had been removed from me.

My sister Christine had marred and had given birth to a little boy, Juanito. They lived at Bracknell near Reading, in a semi-detached house. Just like my parents, I had seen precious little of her over the past few years, but as usually happens with a bereavement in a family, it drew us all closer to another.

On Remembrance Day (November 11th) 1978 I paraded with the band to commemorate that solemn occasion. The day had a bitterly cold feel to it, and the drive to Reading was pretty treacherous, with cars skidding and sliding all over the M4 Motorway. I had travelled with the Bandmaster and one of the French horn players. On arrival at the TA Barracks, I helped the librarian to distribute the march cards and hymn books to the musicians to be used during the parade. At 10.00 hours the band formed up on the square, in readiness to play the regiment onto parade. The band played the regimental march, followed by various marches. After everyone had gathered on parade, they marched to the Cenotaph to commence the Remembrance Day service. At 10.59, the Bugle Call 'Sunset' followed by the Padre...

"At the going down of the Sun, we will remember them."

The one minute's silence followed, after that 'Reveille', then prayers and hymns. Finally, the march back to the square, where the CO gave the parade permission to 'Dismiss!' To complete the occasion, a buffet luncheon had been laid on, and of course, the bar had been opened. Apart from the freezing cold, the Ceremony had gone off according to plan and the CO of the TA Barracks thanked everyone concerned.

In May 1979, I went to camp with the TA for the last time. The band was going to St George's Barracks, Portsmouth. I did not have a job at the time, so getting time off work didn't create a problem. Pauline and I had been shopping and I was about to finish my packing, ready for the journey.

"Where are my car keys?" I asked Pauline.

"In your pocket, I suppose," she answered, knowing what I was like for misplacing things.

"Oh dear, I must have locked them in the Datsun," I said frustratedly.

The car had self-locking doors and as I peered through the driver's window, I could see the keys sticking out of the ignition. I went back into the house.

"Can I borrow yours, Darling?" I asked her.

"They are in my handbag," she replied, then... "and you know where is, don't you?"

"It's in the car!" we shouted in unison.

I rang the local Police-Station. The desk sergeant showed real understanding.

"I will ask one of the constables if he has a key to fit the Datsun. Give me your address and if we have any luck, someone will come to your house.

Thirty minutes later there came a knock at the door. I opened it to find two uniformed police officers on the doorstep.

"I'm sorry Sir, but we haven't got a key to fit your car," one of the officers informed me, "although if you have a coathanger handy, my friend here will show you how to open the door."

It took only minutes to gain access to the car. The policeman used a bent coat-hanger to open the quarter-light window at the rear and then, putting his arm through it, pulled up the self-locking knob and opened the door.

"You can see how easy it is for a burglar to break into a car, can't you?" he said, grinning from ear to ear.

I thanked them both, then loaded up the car ready for my journey.

The week's camp at Eastleigh (Portsmouth this time, not Nairobi!) would unfortunately turn out to be my last with the Terriers. And out of all the camps I had taken part in, it turned out to be the worst! The journey consisted of traffic hold-ups, detours and to top it all, I lost my way a couple of times, so by the time I arrived at the camp, I felt completely exhausted. The Barracks belonged to the Navy, but the building looked identical to the ones used by the Army and Air Force. We musicians settled into our rooms (three to a room) and after taking a meal, went for a stroll. We found a pub locally, then settled down to have a few pints and a game of darts.

On the Monday morning, the sound of Reveille being played roused us at 0630 and after we had breakfasted, we prepared ourselves for the day's duties.

"Gather around lads," the Bandmaster said, "We're on parade on the square in thirty minutes."

My friend Dave and I looked at one another.

"Surely we are not going to have a repetition of last year's camp, Peter?" he exclaimed.

"Looks like it," I replied, "Frank has informed me that we are going to have the doubtful privilege of having our very own Marine RSM to take us for marching drill!"

"Oh, big deal!" my friend answered, sourly.

The band lined up outside the barrack block, then marched onto the square. After tuning up, selecting march cards and sorting out our dressing, we played the Regiment onto parade with their own 2nd Wessex march past.

Everything went according to plan until the RSM inspected the band, as deputising VIP. The musicians of the 2nd Wessex had always been extremely proud of their appearance. We didn't deem it necessary to be instructed to have a haircut, not indeed to press our uniforms. The RSM completed his inspection, then turned to the Bandmaster, saluted and said.

"Sir, with all due respect, most of your musicians need haircuts!" Frank had been made up to the rank of captain prior to going to camp, so was well within his rights to tell the RSM what he thought of his remark, but did not do so. After the parade Frank spoke to the band.

"You heard the Regimental Sergeant Major, lads," then continued, "We had better make our way to the barber's shop."

Being an NCO now, I approached my immediate superior, the band sergeant.

"Ron," I said, "This is ridiculous. You couldn't wish for a more conscientious crowd than our lads."

The sergeant agreed with me completely.

"You're right Peter," he said, "But we don't want to start off the week on the wrong foot, do we?"

For the first time in the whole of my service career, both in the regulars and in the TA, I refused to obey an order. My hair had been cut much shorter than normal, and I did not wish to look like a convict. Also, like myself, one or two of the other lads refused to wear their hair any shorter, so nothing further would be mentioned on the subject!

The band performed at a few non-military functions, one of them being a fête in aid of charity. The band coach had almost arrived at the field in which the fête would be held but Suddenly, it came to a halt. There wasn't enough room for it to pass underneath the entrance arch. A double-decker had been hired in error, so it had to park almost a mile away from the venue. It had been raining rather heavily and this caused a problem. We had to carry our instruments, stands and music across a muddy field to the fête. By the time we had arrived and set up ready to play, we were covered in mud and feeling extremely uncomfortable.

Apart from that, the afternoon went well, and the fête raised £2000 for Children in Need.

On the Thursday evening, we played for an Officer's Mess dinner in 'Pompey'. The coach dropped us musicians off early, so we were able to have a few pints before the event.

The week passed by quickly, the only function remaining being the 'colours' parade, which would be held on the Saturday morning on the last day of camp. After the parade, we musicians were free to return home.

By July 1980 I had handed in my uniforms and kit. It made me feel rather sad to be leaving my friends, but with a

152-mile round trip each Tuesday, returning home at 3am, and up for work at 0730 it became too much for me!

By September of the same year, after three months of being unemployed, I had taken a job with Molins, a cigarette-making machine manufacturers at Milton Keynes. I only had a clerical job, but with a family to support, it had to be better than no job at all. Another big event took place in January 1981 – the birth of our second child, Amanda Jane, who weighed in at 9lbs 2oz.

Poor old me, I still kept trying…

I advertised for musicians with a view to starting a big dance band, but after auditioning dozens of musicians and singers I had progressed no further forward to achieving my ambition. For a short while, I played with another Tyrolean group, but that didn't last long.

Then I had an idea – one of many I had over the years – of using the students from the School of Music at Stantonbury. I went along one Saturday morning to listen to the student orchestra rehearsing: On the stage appeared a large selection of pupils between the ages of 9 and 10 years. The junior orchestra sounded excellent, but the children were too young for the band I needed. During one of those visits I met David Wilkinson, an extremely versatile musician. David had played Dixieland Jazz on the clarinet for years, with great proficiency, also being the Deputy Headmaster at Bedford High School and, in complete contrast, in charge of the wind band (similar to a military band, but on a smaller scale) in his spare time.

I joined in with the clarinet section and it pleased me to be able to give the students the benefit of my experience. David shared my excitement at the idea of starting a Dance Band. The PBSO started with just a handful of musicians: myself leading the band on alto sax, clarinet and vocals, David on 2nd alto and clarinet, Chris on 1st trumpet, Paul on piano and string bass, Robin on 1st trombone, Helen on 2nd trombone and Tony Lock on drums.

'The Pete Bradbury Swing Orchestra' may have been a fancy name, but the Hatters didn't seem quite appropriate for that type of band. Apart from David and myself, the others were teenagers and did not have any previous experience of jazz or dance band music, but were excellent readers of music. Under my direction and with help from David, the band soon began to take shape.

Every once in a while, we introduced a new student into the band. After six months had passed, the line-up looked more impressive: two alto saxes, two tenor saxes, piano, bass, drums, three trombones, one trumpet, bass and rhythm guitars. An even match of boys and girls made sure that no one complained of bias.

They were an exceptionally keen bunch of youngsters, and as the quality of the band improved I felt able to accept a few engagements. The first one was an end of term concert at the School of Music at Stantonbury, just a five-minute spot to begin with. The early part of the concert included solo performances by children as young as ten and was most entertaining. Now came the turn of the PBSO. We opened with our signature tune 'Debbie', followed by 'Misty', then 'Shake Rattle and Twist', followed by 'Moonlight Serenade' and finally 'Debbie' once more to end the performance. I felt really delighted, and had visions of my band doing really well!

The Band met every Monday evening for rehearsal. I rushed home from work at Olivetti Typewriters and Computers, had my evening meal, then dashed to Stantonbury to set up the practice room, ready for rehearsal. It may have been hard work, but I really did have an objective in life to aim for now. I placed adverts in the local papers and shops and made many phone calls in an effort to encourage new recruits. One way and another, it cost me a lot of money, but I had the grim determination to produce a proficient Dance Band.

In the summer of 1983, a forthcoming event at Ousedale School, Newport Pagnell caught my eye. They were organising a fête to raise funds for a new school mini-bus. All proceeds would be going to finance that. I wrote to the Headmaster, offering the services of the band, hoping that once in the public eye, we would be offered further engagements. I received a reply stating that the Headmaster would be grateful for my offer, and enclosed details of the programme. At the following rehearsal I announced that the band would be playing at the fête. The musicians received the news with enthusiasm, so between us we worked out the programme of music. After agreeing to the selection of music that we were going to play, David spoke up.

"We are still short of one or two musicians. We have a full sax section, apart from a baritone. The three trombones will be sufficient, but what about trumpets?"

I thought hard before answering.

"As usual Dave, we have an imbalance, I don't know why, but we don't seem to be able to attract any trumpet players."

"If Chris didn't come I really don't know how we would carry on." Dave replied.

Unfortunately Dave had 'hit the nail on the head'. Only on two separate occasions had there been a full trumpet section – once for a recording and once for a concert.

The afternoon of the concert arrived. The sun shone brightly, but a ferocious wind blew. It would be the first time the band had performed outside of the Music School and the young musicians were rather tentative about it.

"Don't be nervous," I reassured them, "You have all worked hard and I know that you will be a success."

And, apart from the wind blowing the music stands over, it certainly did turn out to be a success!

I had managed to borrow two trumpeters from a local brass band, and a rhythm guitarist from Luton. Some of the musicians had travelled a long way at their own expense, but that reflected the spirit of the band. At the end of the afternoon the headmaster thanked us for our contribution to the day; £2000 had been raised towards the purchase of the school mini-bus and, along wit the proceeds from other functions, this would be enough for their requirements.

I felt on top of the world. I had a permanent job, my family, a house, a car and to make my life complete, I had my own band…

Unfortunately (as usual), it wasn't going to last. During September 1984 I was made redundant yet again, which left me in the position of having to search for another job. Pauline comforted me, reminding me that I still had her and the children, plus our home (which we were purchasing via a mortgage). I realised that she made sense, of course, and that I would find another job. I only remained out of work until January 1985, then secured a temporary position with Filtrona Cigarette Components, at Bletchley, which lasted until July 1986, when I started a job at Olivetti Computers, that lasted me up until September 1989.

After the fête at Ousedale School, even though it had been a success, the musicians began to let me down. After a hard day, I used to dash home, sometimes giving advice to students on how to play their parts, then rush to rehearsal. Arriving there to find two, three, or sometimes only four people had turned up disheartened me somewhat. Of course David always turned up, as did Chris on trumpet (I could always rely on him) and Tony the drummer. What a peculiar quartet: two alto saxophones, a trumpet and a drummer!

The 'writing was on the wall' for the band and I just couldn't understand what had happened.

Soon after the Ousedale School fête I met the manager of Woughton Campus at Milton Keynes. After seeing my advert in the local paper for a Big Band Concert at Stantonbury campus, he came along to hear the band. What he heard certainly impressed him, and told me so. We had a twenty-two piece band at Stantonbury campus that evening. Due to advertising in the papers, contacting the Musicians Union, and making numerous telephone calls, I had my complete band for the first time. The line-up was five saxes, four trumpets, four trombones, piano, bass, drums, bass and rhythm guitars, plus four extra musicians.

The musicians had travelled from as far away as Bedford (13 miles) and Luton (25 miles) just to play with the PBSO. A reporter and photographer from the local paper came along and I stood in front of the band (my band), feeling extremely proud and excited. The second trumpeter's father had brought along his tape-recorder so we could listen to our performance at a later date.

I picked up my clarinet to lead the band into our signature tune, 'Debbie'.

The photographer snapped pictures of the band during the course of the evening and during the interval Mark, the Manager of Woughton Campus, approached me.

"I would like your band to play at my place one evening," he said, "How much would you charge?"

"We are only an amateur band," I replied, "but expenses would be useful."

"Give me a ring and we'll discuss it," Mark continued, then finally, "I have to go now, as I have to be on duty at 9 o'clock."

Apart from a few mishaps, the evening had been a success. The hall had been comparatively empty, but the few people who had sat down to listen, clapped and said that it had been a pleasant change.

I managed to keep the PBSO going, although there were certain evenings when I felt like 'calling it a day'. The band had its final public performance at Woughton Campus and although my hopes had been raised many times before, they were going to be dashed yet again. The chairs had been laid out in rows and the audience were taking their seats, waiting patiently for the band to start playing. As usual I had had to 'beg, borrow, and steal' in an effort to produce a complete band for the show. Unfortunately we were a few members short, but I had managed to find replacements, as usual, the main problem being a lack of trumpet players, and in addition I had to make do with an electric keyboard player and string bass player who were inexperienced at reading music. At last the PBSO had set up and ready to perform.

"Oh, my goodness," I said. "Where is the drummer?"

It was unbelievable. At the last moment my regular drummer Ken had to go abroad on business. I had contacted a deputy, but he had not arrived.

"Can you believe it, Dave?" I asked my friend, "A dance band without a drummer – and he is supposed to be a semi-professional musician!"

Dave nodded his head in agreement.

We did mange without a drummer and the evening turned out to be such a success that Mark asked us to play there again. Each musician received £4 expenses – the most that many of the youngsters had ever earned from music.

After that, I tried many ways to make a success of music, but eventually I had to stop 'bashing my head against a brick wall' and turn my attention to other things. I wrote a song for Amanda, 'Amanda Mine', which did not become published. I also wrote children's songs, complete with cartoon drawings.

I even wrote children's stories with drawings, but finally decided that I would write my own autobiography, so I did!

At the same time I decided to write a song that would incorporate 'Children in Need' and 'Christmas'. I called it 'Is it Truly Christmas?' The publishers, unfortunately, were not interested in those songs, but I used 'Amanda' with a band and recorded 'Is it Truly Christmas?' with children (including my daughter Amanda) from the Portfield School, Newport Pagnell. I used 'Is it Truly Christmas' to further promote 'Children in Need' in a Radio Bedford Sports Day for the Charity.

Our third daughter, Rachel Elaine Susan, arrived on New Years Eve 1987, and I decided (as with both her sisters before her) that I would write a song for her. I called it a 'Message to Rachel' and used it for my dissertation when I graduated from University College Chichester in May 2001, attaining a BA Mus (Hons) Degree.

But I had yet to endure one or two more tragedies in my life, within a short while. My best friend of many years, John Steel, died of cancer and my Dad Tommy also died of cancer. Mum died of yellow jaundice and Pauline's Mum died of Diabetes. Finally, Uncle Jim died of natural causes at the ripe old age of 96.

We moved to Bognor Regis in 1997 (leaving Amanda and Debbie behind at Milton Keynes with their respective boyfriends. I joined an Amateur Concert Wind Band, staying with them for three years. It seemed fairly interesting at the time, playing on the bandstands on the seafront and at Hotham Park, also various concerts (mainly for charity).

I had also an amazing experience: Tommy Mcquater (the younger) whom I hadn't seen since we were both aged 12 at Butlins, came to play at our local golf club with a small group. I made myself known to him (it seemed too much of a coincidence for it not to be the same person). His Dad

Tommy, along with my Dad Tommy were two of the original founder members of the Squadronaires Dance Orchestra. I do believe that Ronnie Aldrich, the pianist with the Squadronaires is still living and playing. To the best of my knowledge, they are the only two remaining members of the original orchestra still alive today.

One other exciting thing has happened to me within the past few months. My first-born daughter Caroline contacted me by letter. Both Pauline and I had been trying to find her for years, without success. So I now have a further three grandchildren that I previously didn't know about!

I recently wrote a song for Caroline entitled, 'Hello Again – Hello Blues'.

~ End ~

Middlesex Yeomanry Territorial Army Band Camp,
Tilshead, Wilts, July 1976.